Qigong
for Healing

Dr Choo Cheng Ngiap

TIMES BOOKS INTERNATIONAL
Singapore • Kuala Lumpur

Published 2002 by
Times Books International, an imprint of
Times Media Private Limited
Times Centre, 1 New Industrial Road
Singapore 536196
Tel: (65) 6213 9288
Fax: (65) 6285 4871
E-mail: te@tpl.com.sg
Online Bookstore:
http://www.timesone.com.sg/te

Times Subang
Lot 46, Subang Hi-Tech Industrial Park
Batu Tiga, 40000 Shah Alam
Selangor Darul Ehsan, Malaysia
Fax & Tel: (603) 5636 3517
E-mail: cchong@tpg.com.my

Printed in Singapore

ISBN 981 204 971 1

National Library Board (Singapore) Cataloguing in Publication Data

Choo, Cheng Ngiap.
    Qigong for healing / Choo Cheng Ngiap. – Singapore : Times
Books International, 2002.
    p. cm.

    ISBN : 981-204-971-1

1.   Ch'i kung. I. Title.

RA781.8
613.71 — dc21   SLS2002012773

Table of Contents

Channels, Acupuncture Points, and Meridians

How to Use the Information in this Book

This book is a record of the personal study of patients with different diseases for which modern medicine has not produced positive therapeutic results. Each case had been seen, diagnosed, and treated by trained medical doctors.

This comprehensive presentation of Kong Jing Qigong is for self-learning. However, it is preferable that one learns Kong Jing Qigong under the supervision of a qualified Qigong instructor. If the exercise is intended to treat particular diseases, diagnosis must be made by a doctor before starting the exercise. Medicine given by the doctor must be continued for a time, usually about two months, to tide over the period before Qigong exercise produces results.

Kong Jing Qigong has been practised by about a million people in China without ill effect, according to Grand Master Huang Jen Jong. If there is any adverse effect at the beginning of the exercise, such as chills, headaches, or giddiness, and especially in the first two weeks, the exercise should be discontinued. One should also consult a doctor as well as scrutinise the instructions in the book again.

When instructions concerning preparation prior to exercise as well as the exercise steps are followed correctly, one should feel comfortable, relaxed, and warm. Profuse sweating should occur in about 10 minutes, and this is followed by improved sleep and gastrointestinal function.

For newcomers to Qigong and for those unfamiliar with certain specialized terms:
1. The glossary on page 140 explains the medical terms used in the book.
2. Channels (e.g. lung, spleen, etc.) and qi points (e.g. Laogong P8) are essential to the text. A list of illustrations of the channels is provided on page 3. The points, which are captioned in these illustrations, are also listed in the index to the book, in bold type.
3. All references to the masculine gender are for convenience and include both males and females.

How to Use the Exercise VCD with the Book

The book should be read and understood thoroughly before starting on the exercises. When you are ready to begin exercising, the VCD will guide you through the following:

Swinging Arms Exercise: Relaxation
Horse Stance Posture: Building Qi
Winding Up Exercise
Embracing the Moon: Biofeedback of Qi
Fostering Primordial Qi: Rejuvenation
Holding the Ball with Both Hands
Holding the Ball with Fingering
Rolling the Ball
Rolling the Ball with Fingering
Regulating Qi through Three Entry Points

Acknowledgements

It is difficult for a student of modern medical science to accept another medical discipline, especially one that has little scientific support at present, even though it has been practised for thousands of years in China. I owe it to Diana Chan Oi Yee that I was finally able to summon up the courage to go to Taiwan in 1976 to study acupuncture. I am very thankful to my wife, Diana, and I am proud to dedicate this book to her.

I am greatly obliged to Grand Master Huang Jen Jong of Shanghai, China, for allowing me to make use of Kong Jing Qigong. He has helped greatly in the preparation of this book.

Grand Master Huang Jen Jong

Grand Master Huang Jen Jong is one of the well-known contemporary Qigong masters in China. He started his Qigong school 20 years ago and he has more than a million students in China. His students have also spread to Japan, Malaysia and Singapore.

He compiled the book *Kong Jing Qigong* which was based on the books *Treatments of the Magic Palm* and *The Internal Qigong Exercise* written by Da Mol of the Shaolin Monastery. Using his book, Master Huang taught his students how to keep themselves healthy and to practise self-treatment for some chronic diseases. He also taught his students how to use their qi to treat sickness in other people.

In 1984, he established a Kong Jing Qigong Academy in Shen Jiunn, China, for teaching and for therapeutic purposes.

I am grateful to Master Huang for allowing me to use his Kong Jing Qigong in my book *Qigong for Healing*.

Dr Choo Cheng Ngiap

Dr Choo Cheng Ngiap is a member of the Malaysian College of General Practitioners. He graduated from Hong Kong University and has been in private medical practice for more than 30 years. He is also a Doctor of Medicine for Medica Alternativa.

Dr Choo studied acupuncture in the Chinese Acupuncture Research Centre in Taiwan. He has practised Qigong in many different schools, and for nearly 10 years has concentrated on the study of Kong Jing Qigong for the treatment of diseases. This book is based on his knowledge of Kong Jing Qigong and its application in curing chronic fatigue syndrome, migraine, sinusitis, and other conditions, without side effects.

Dr Choo may be contacted by email at chooby@pd.jaring.my, or by fax at 02-082-250533.

Preface

This book centres on the use of Qigong exercise in the treatment of disease. It approaches the subject of Qigong from the standpoint of a medical practitioner, aiming to situate this ancient Chinese technique in the context of western medical theory and to illustrate its usefulness in the treatment of chronic disease. As such, it will prove useful to students and practitioners of acupuncture, students of Qigong, and all those interested in improving their health or relieving health problems such as chronic fatigue syndrome, migraines, and chronic sinusitis.

It is my personal experience of working with patients suffering from these chronic diseases that has prompted me to write this book. Having had the pleasure of helping patients who had been abandoned by western medicine, enabling them to regain their health within a period of months, I wish to share this knowledge with others for whom western medicine has been unable to provide a cure. I have found Qigong therapy to be a useful supplement to both western medical techniques and acupuncture, particularly in the treatment of chronic disease.

Qigong has been used by Chinese masters for thousands of years, and is currently practised by approximately one million Chinese as an aid in improving health and increasing longevity. It is a safe and effective exercise if practised properly. This book provides a reference for self-learning this valuable art. As long as the instructions are carefully followed, Qigong exercise should present no risk to the student. However, it is preferable to learn Qigong under the supervision of a qualified Qigong instructor, if at all possible, especially if exercise is intended to treat medical conditions. If you suffer from a medical condition, consult a qualified medical practitioner before starting any exercise program. Be sure to consult your doctor before discontinuing any medication.

When the instructions are followed carefully and correct posture is maintained, you should feel comfortable, relaxed, and warm during exercise. After 10 minutes, you will begin to sweat profusely. You should experience no discomfort or pain. If, however, you suffer from any ill effects, such as chills, headaches, or dizziness, especially during the first two weeks of practice, discontinue exercise and consult a doctor.

Chapter 1

Introduction

In the past few decades, with increased knowledge about health and medicine, people have become more aware of the ill effects of drugs and pollution, and the limitations of modern medicine and treatment, and are in search of an alternative therapy. Qigong and acupuncture, which are based on a different medical philosophy, are being used more and more to fill this gap.

Qigong and acupuncture constitute the great contributions to the medical field by Chinese medicine in the past few thousand years. Together with herbs, chemicals, moxibustion, and surgery, they have played a major role in the maintenance of health and the treatment of disease for the Chinese in a recorded history of five thousand years.

One of the earliest books on Qigong was written by the famous Chinese surgeon Hua Tuo between A.D. 160 and 190. He was the first person to use anaesthesia in an operation, combining five types of herbs to be taken orally before surgery. This was later introduced to Japan and the Arab countries. Qigong exercise, which he formulated, imitates the movement of five animals. He taught it to the people to maintain their health.

Qigong is an exercise used to cultivate and control a person's energy. It is an energy skill designed to increase energy resources and to enhance health and vitality. Qigong serves as a form of preventive as well as curative health care. It works through the energy channel system to balance yin and yang energy and promote the formation of hormones, the assimilation of nutrition, and the formation of immunological elements in the blood.

The basis of Traditional Chinese medicine is different from that of western medicine. Their approaches to the problems of health and sickness also differ. To learn Qigong or to understand acupuncture treatment, one must have a basic understanding of Chinese medical theory.

The Foundation Stone of Chinese Medicine

The central thesis of Traditional Chinese medicine is the principle of *qi*, which means energy. The Chinese consider qi to be the source of life. It is the life force, which governs growth and health. Qi is responsible for the life process and the functioning of all organs in the human body. The state of health of the body depends on the strength or weakness of this energy. It circulates in the body in a closed circuit running from organ to organ in a definite network of channels called the *jing luoh*, which are located in the connective tissue sheets, called fascia. The fascia are located in the vicinity of the main blood vessels and nerves throughout the body. In a recent scientific study qi was found to be composed of electricity and infrared radiation. Through its flowing movement, qi produces an electromagnetic force to pull the electrically charged blood cells along the blood vessels and thus influence the circulation of the blood. Thus we can say that qi is the commander of the blood, as has been observed by Chinese physicians in the past. Together with blood, it supplies nutrition to the body and maintains the systems in the body in a state of homeostasis, thus creating favourable conditions for body health.

The smooth and strong running of qi and blood is a prerequisite for good health. In modern medicine, obstructed blood flow can give rise to pathological changes in the affected tissue and, depending on the severity of the blockage, can cause pain due to transient ischaemic change, or necrosis if the blockage is more severe. When this obstruction occurs in the brain, the affected brain cells die, causing hemiplegia, or paralysis of one side of the body. In the heart, it results in a heart attack. In the toe, this causes gangrene, and the affected toe may have to be amputated. In traditional Chinese medicine, qi is the leader of blood. Where qi goes, blood is always led to flow. If the flow of qi is stagnant, blood circulation will be obstructed and the person will fall sick. A famous physician who lived two thousand years ago said, "When qi is flowing smoothly, no sickness will occur."

Yin and Yang, the Polarity of Qi

Unlike blood flow, which can be blocked due to the weak pumping force of the heart, the reduced size of the blood vessels, and the loss of elasticity in degenerated vessels, qi circulation through the ionized liquid in the fascia only becomes stagnant when its force is weakened or the polarity of the energy becomes unbalanced. Qi has yin and yang phases, similar to positive and negative charges for electricity. Chinese medicine places great emphasis on this polarity, and considers yin and yang as two complementary poles of energy. They are reciprocal states of cyclic change in the rhythmic transformation of energy. Yin and yang phases are relative rather than absolute. They always counteract each other and seek to strike the most stable balance.

Transmutation is a fundamental law of qi circulation. The predominantly yin qi of the lung channel travels from the lung along the arm to the thumb. From there it crosses over to the index finger and transforms itself into predominantly yang qi, coursing along the large intestine channel from the arm to the head. From the head the stomach channel continues with yang qi to the spleen channel, where the qi is transformed to yin again. The same dynamic process continues from channel to channel in a closed circuit similar to alternating electric current, from negative to positive and back to negative and so on, continuously creating a dynamic force for the qi circulation throughout the body. The theory of yin and yang postulates that there exists in everything a relationship of mutually opposing and unifying phases of qi. In the human body, growth and physiological and pathological changes are the result of this process. Excessive yin will cause yang sickness, and an excess of yang will result in yin sickness. Thus the destruction of yin and yang balance is the cause of sickness.

An energy imbalance can cause fever, intestinal upsets, headache, high blood pressure, and other disorders. If such conditions are not corrected, they will lead to degeneration and death. If the imbalance is corrected in time, health will be regained.

Healing with Qigong

Acupuncture and Qigong exercises are two methods created by Chinese physicians to regulate qi circulation and thus reestablish health. Acupuncture makes use of needles to stimulate acupuncture points along the channels in the body. Qigong exercise is more complex and requires the patient to actively practise exercises to cultivate qi. This involves relaxation of the mind and body, with slow breathing and precise movements and postures of the body. It builds up the life energy to be stored in the mesentery and diaphragm, and encourages qi circulation. Qigong can be used to build up qi to be transmitted to other people for therapeutic purposes. Through Qigong exercise, yin and yang energy becomes more balanced, the functioning of the organs is enhanced, and the circulation of qi and blood becomes smooth and strong, thus helping to prevent or treat sickness, attain normal health, and increase life expectancy.

Traditional Chinese medicine served the Chinese people well until the nineteenth century, when the British introduced modern western medicine after the Opium War of 1837. Traditional Chinese medicine was overshadowed for more than a hundred years. In the early 1970s, there was a revival of international interest in acupuncture after the visit of US President Nixon to China. What caught the general attention were the analgesic and anaesthetic effects of acupuncture and Qigong. There followed a surge of enthusiasm among western-trained doctors to learn this ancient art of healing. Many seminars and teaching courses were organized. Unfortunately, these were either too elementary, too short, or oversimplified. About this time, endorphins were discovered in the brain, and receptors of endorphins were found in the brain and the intestine. Endorphins are very similar to morphine in their capacity for pain relief. This offered a very good explanation for the analgesic and anaesthetic effects of acupuncture and Qigong, which were found to stimulate the production of endorphins in the body.

So much attention has been focused on this particular function that many people are not aware of the other important uses of acupuncture and Qigong, which include sedation, homeostasis, immunity enhancement, motor recovery of paralysed muscles, and anti-inflammatory function. Many of us unconsciously have attempted to assimilate the therapeutic effects of acupuncture and Qigong into modern medical philosophy, which has resulted in missing the forest for the trees. Modern medicine tends to be specific, dealing with bacteria and organs individually, whereas traditional Chinese medicine is holistic, approaching the situation as a whole. It treats sickness by bringing all the organs in the body to their maximum capacity, which in turn enhances immune function.

Acupuncture and Qigong both depend on the healing power of qi to treat disease. Acupuncture is best suited to acute cases that need immediate attention, such as infection and inflammation. Qigong exercise takes time to build up qi that is strong enough to produce therapeutic effects, and is therefore more suitable for chronic diseases. However, in acute cases the combination of acupuncture with external qi from Qigong was found to enhance therapeutic effects tremendously. In my experience, it works particularly well in dental abscesses, sinusitis, and infectious conjunctivitis. For chronic problems, such as migraine, rhinitis, sinusitis, bronchitis, rheumatoid arthritis, low backache, and chronic fatigue syndrome, I taught my patients to practise Qigong every day. The results were quite remarkable: within two months they started to feel the effects.

The Qigong exercise I taught my patients was very simple. The main theme of the exercise is to relax the body mentally and physically and to build up and strengthen the qi in the body. This regulates qi and establishes a balance between yin and yang polarities. The circulation of qi and blood is accelerated, and the functioning of all the organs in the body is improved. With the brain as the coordinating centre, through the biofeedback mechanism of qi and hormones, the body is able to enhance its immune function to combat sickness and bring the body back to normal health.

The holistic therapeutic effect is particularly useful as a supplement to the treatment of some chronic diseases. There were cases of hypertension that had been resistant to treatment, where the person practised Qigong for other ailments and found that his blood pressure came down satisfactorily while taking the same medication. A diabetic who practised Qigong could reduce the dosage of his medicine, and regained his grip. He was also freed from cramps in his calves. Many cases of failing eyesight and hearing improved. Mental concentration, reading speed, and temperament, too, have improved with Qigong exercise.

After many years of experience in Qigong exercise as a healing power, I cannot help but marvel at its therapeutic result. It is not so much that it serves as a medical alternative that can produce the same effects as modern medicine; what has fascinated me is what it can do that modern medicine fails to achieve. Ménière's syndrome and chronic fatigue syndrome are two solid examples. It is this fact that inspires me to write this book to introduce this ancient art of healing to my fellows and to share the benefits of Qigong with you.

There are many schools of Qigong that are beneficial to health. In this book I specifically chose to focus on Kong Jing Qigong because it is easy to learn, quick in building up qi, and suitable for the weak and sick. Kong Jing Qigong consists of elementary, intermediate, and senior courses. In this book, I emphasize mainly the teaching of the elementary course, as it is geared toward improving health and curing disease. The intermediate and senior courses are mainly for treating sickness through external qi.

Teaching Yourself

The main aim of this book is to teach Kong Jing Qigong for self-treatment. It can be used for independent learning and practice. It is also invaluable to those who have learned and are still practising Kong Jing Qigong to master the correct procedures of the exercise and to understand how this exercise can treat their sickness.

Although Kong Jing Qigong can be learned from this book, it is better to follow a good instructor in Kong Jing Qigong and make use of this book as a reference. This exercise depends very much on correct posture and fingering, and practitioners are usually not able to perceive their own mistakes. Above all, for people who are learning Qigong to treat their own sicknesses, an experienced Qigong master will be able to answer their questions regarding any reactions that may occur during Qigong exercise. Often, students who have been practising Kong Jing Qigong for more than a year with an instructor still make mistakes in posturing due to a lack of understanding of the principles involved.

In Kong Jing Qigong exercise, there is a set of procedures to be followed. The first step is to build up the qi by putting all the skeletal muscles into contraction to produce qi in the form of electricity. When the qi becomes strong (with one to two months of daily practice, each lasting for 30 to 45 minutes), it is fed back from the palms through the jing luoh channels to the organs in the body. This gives a boosting force to the qi in the channels. By the movements of the arms and the flexing of the fingers in different postures, qi circulation is further strengthened in each channel. Transmutation of the polarity of the qi in different levels of yin and yang in the channels is achieved. Eventually all systems in the body are stabilized, secretion of hormones and enzymes is stimulated, immunity is enhanced, the immune system is harmonized, and the body repairing system motivated to control disease. The treatment is therefore termed self-treatment, and the method is holistic, treating the whole body system as a single unit.

Chapter 2

Qi, Vital Energy

In modern health science, the human life process is carried out through two important systems: the central nervous system and the blood circulatory system. The central nervous system is the control centre of the various organs in the body. It consists of the brain and its peripheral nervous system. These control intelligent activity, the senses, the will, and motion, as well as such important activities as respiration, blood circulation, secretion of digestive hormones, and sexual activity. The blood circulatory system consists of the heart and the blood vessels. They carry nutrition to every part of the body, and also carry away the waste products of metabolism for purification. The blood cells also play an important part in defending the body against sickness. When these two systems stop functioning, life comes to an end.

The Chinese in the past four thousand years have established another system, which is totally different from the two recognized systems of modern medicine. The foundation of this system is the existence of qi, or bioenergy, in the human body. If the central nervous system and the cardiovascular system together with other organs in the body can be compared to the separate machines in a factory, qi can then be considered to be the electric power. When the power circuit is connected, all the machines start to work. If the electric current is turned off, all the machines stop functioning. Therefore, in Chinese medical philosophy the death of a person is due to the termination of qi circulation in the body, and not to the malfunctioning of an individual system or organ.

Qi is not only the main element in Chinese medicine on which the life or death of a person is based. It is also considered to be the fundamental element that forms all things in the world. Our body is therefore surrounded by different kinds of environmental external qi, which include radiation from the cosmos, the magnetic field of the earth, climatic changes (wind, heat, dryness, and wetness), and a lot of artificial aberrant energies, like electromagnetic radiation from microwaves, high tension electric currents, televisions, atomic radiation, etc. Some of them are very harmful to our bodies.

What is Qi?

The original Chinese character for qi (炁) means energy. The upper part of the word means *nothing* or *emptiness* and indicates that qi is invisible and cannot be held or touched. The lower part of the word means *fire*, something that gives rise to energy in the form of heat. Thus qi is energy that is invisible and cannot be touched. It can be felt, however. If a person is in good health, he can feel the presence of qi by putting both hands in front of the body, palms facing each other about 6 inches (16 cm) apart. The hands are open with fingers extended but relaxed. The space between the fingers is equal to half a finger width. After about 60 seconds, he will be able to feel heat, and then a pulling and repelling force when he moves his palms. This is qi in the form of infrared radiation and electromagnetic force.

FEELING THE QI

Hold your hands with palms facing each other on a vertical line about 6 inches (16 cm) apart. Hold this position for one minute. The qi coming from the centre of the palms at Laogong P8 point can be felt as a pulling force, making the palms feel numb and bloated. If you have trouble feeling the qi, move your hands back and forth in a rubbing motion to help them feel the electromagnetic force.

The hands can also be held in a horizontal position, again 6 inches (16 cm) apart. Hold for one minute. To strengthen the feeling of qi in the palms, slowly bring them closer or pull them slightly apart.

TESTING YOUR QI

Use a thin metal chain with a small metal ring attached to one end. Hold one end of the chain between the right thumb and index finger, letting the ring hang down. Disengage the rest of the fingers. Rest your right elbow on a table, and relax the muscles of the right arm and hand. Keep your eyes focused on the ring while you are performing the test, and hold your arm and hand steady. After 1 to 3 minutes, the ring will start to swing back and forth with the strength of the qi.

 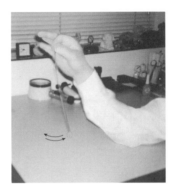

You can also use this method to test whether a particular food is suitable for you. Place the food on the table and hold the chain as above. Keep your eyes focused on the food as you perform the test. After a while, energy from your hand will be conducted down the chain to the food, while energy from the food will rise to meet this energy at the ring. If the food is a suitable one for you, the ring will swing in a clockwise direction. Unsuitable foods will make the ring swing in a counterclockwise direction.

During Qigong exercise, a person can feel qi circulation like a warm stream flowing in the body. It may resemble itchiness, bloating, an insect bite, or electric shock and numbness. When acupuncture is performed for a patient using electrical stimulation, the patient can feel the presence of qi if he puts his palm over the pulsating needle on the channel. It feels like an electromagnetic force striking his palms. From the above demonstration, it is clear that every living person has qi circulating in the body and is able to emit external qi. The amount of qi is weak compared with someone who has practised Qigong, but it is strong enough to treat small ailments. Old Chinese women very often use it to relieve abdominal colic or constipation in babies by massaging the babies' abdomen with their palms, rubbing in a clockwise direction. The qi transmitted through their palms will relieve intestinal spasms and increase peristalsis, thus stopping the abdominal pain and relieving constipation. The qi in the palms must be strong to be used externally. The strength of qi can easily be determined by the warmth of the palms. A cold palm is not of much use.

Types of Qi

Qi may be classified into two main groups according to function.

- **Managing qi:** This is the qi that runs in the circuit of channels in the body. It serves to regulate qi in the channels and bring nutrition to the organs.
- **Guarding qi:** This flows under the skin in the superficial fascia. Together with the skin, it provides a protective shield against invasion by organisms such as bacteria, virus, fungus, insects, and parasites, and aberrant *sie qi*, the evil energy from extreme weather conditions such as heat, cold, damp, dryness, wind, etc. It is a common experience in the tropics for people who are caught in a drizzle under the hot sun to end up with a headache and a cold. It is the chilling effect of the rain, which breaks through body resistance to create an opening for the virus to cause an upper respiratory infection.

How Qi is Formed

Qi is formed from many sources, which can be divided into external and internal origins.

External Sources

- The qi of grains comes from the food we consume. It is digested in the stomach and intestines by the action of enzymes, which release nutrition and energy and convey them to the organs.
- Oxygen from the air in ionised form reacts with the qi of grains and forms essential qi in the lungs, from where it drives the qi in the channels.
- Cosmic radiation from the sun, moon, stars, and planets, which forms a thick electromagnetic field enclosing the earth and induces an electromagnetic force in our body through the head Baihui G20 point in the Governor meridian (Du Mai). The electromagnetic force from the earth enters our body through the perineum.

THE CIRCULATION OF QI

Qi circulation starts from the lung channel. The lungs receive ionized particles from the air, which combine with the essence of food carried in the blood from the intestines to form *chung qi*, or essence of qi. Chung qi, along with the breathing movement of the lungs, provides the driving force for the circulation of qi. Qi flow moves on to the large intestine, stomach, and spleen channels, following from the chest to the thumb, from the fingertips to the head, from the head to the toes, and from the toes to the trunk, thus completing one round of circulation. This is followed by a second circuit through the heart, small intestine, bladder, kidney, pericardium, triple warmer, gall bladder, and liver channels, repeating the same pattern of flow from body to fingers to head to toes and back to the body.

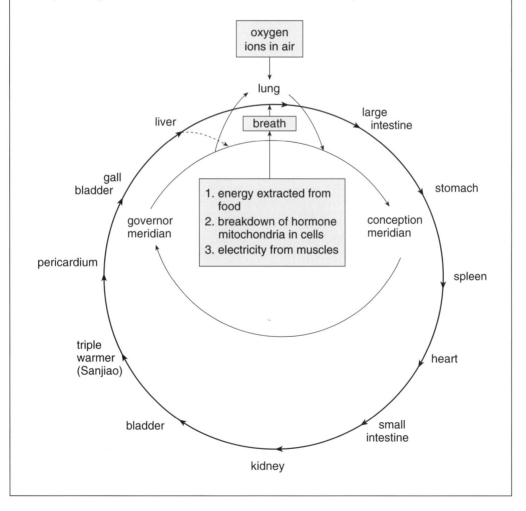

Internal Sources

- Most of the energy in the body is produced by the mitochondria in the cells. Energy production in cells begins when oxidation of food causes high energy electrons to pair along the electron transport chains and fall to successively lower levels. Part of the energy released pumps hydrogen ions out of the mitochondria, and the resulting gradient of ions drives the production of ATP, a small molecule that provides energy for most of the many processes in the rest of the cell. The breakdown of DNA (deoxyribonucleic acid) also releases energy from the nucleus of the cells. This is particularly important in the brain.
- The flowing stream of blood in the vessels produces electric current.
- Electricity is produced by muscle contractions. This phenomenon is used in Qigong exercise to build up qi.

All the above elements contribute to the formation of qi, which in scientific studies in the past few decades has been found to consist of infrared and electromagnetic radiation, and microparticle flow.

Electricity Produced by Muscle Contraction

The concept of electricity produced by the muscles was inspired by the electric eel. The eel is a native freshwater fish of South America. As a defence, the eel can produce 650 volts of electric shock—strong enough to stun a man in the water. Nine feet (3 m) long and weighing about 49 pounds (22 kg), the eel's tail region contains an electrical organ composed of muscle cells that have changed their function to the discharging and storing of electric charges. Its electric plate is composed of a layer of fascia with a layer of muscle fibres, which form a fine gelatinous layer directly under the soft, naked skin of the fish. The electric plates are connected to the central nervous system through the nerves in the spinal cord. The eel can, therefore, discharge electric current at will.

In human muscles, contractivity is developed to a high degree by the muscle cells, which are composed of a protoplasmic substance. Muscle is excitable. It responds to external stimuli by contracting and by coordinating the various groups of muscles, producing movement under nervous control. Each contraction of muscle fibre is associated with an electrical charge that can be measured.

In a resting state, the interior of the heart muscle cell is negatively charged with respect to the exterior. When the muscle cell is stimulated by a nerve impulse, it starts to contract. With each contraction, there occurs a rapid reversal of charge. The interior of the cell becomes electrically positive with respect to its exterior. This electrical charge, which occurs at the same time as the rhythmic activity of cardiac muscle fibres, is similar to those seen in non-rhythmic structures, such as the skeletal and visceral muscles and neurons, when these tissues are excited naturally or artificially.

Somatic muscle plays an important part in the production of electrical charges and heat. Even when they are not producing active movement, they are maintained in a state of partial contraction by the constant arrival of nervous impulses, and thus the electrical charges continue even when the muscles are seemingly at rest.

There are two types of electrical charges – positive and negative. Two objects of similar charge exert a force of repulsion on each other. Two of opposite charges attract each other. Any movement of electrically charged elements, such as subatomic charged particles (e.g. electrons having negative charge, protons having positive charge) or ions (atoms that have lost or gained one or more electrons), produces electrical current.

Blood cells and plasma contain electrically charged particles called ions. Blood is forced through rhythmical contractions of the heart to circulate in the vascular system. It forces the electrically charged carriers, the blood cells and the plasma, to circulate in the blood vessels, thus generating electrical current.

Kong Jing Qigong makes use of this electricity generated by contracting muscles to build up qi in the body. The muscles of the four limbs, which constitute the bulk of body muscle, are kept in contraction through the maintenance of a certain posture. Bioelectricity is thus produced and stored in the diaphragm and the mesentery in the abdomen for use when the store is fully charged, very similar to charging a car battery by running the engine. The procedure by which qi is produced in Qigong exercise is called the fundamental exercise. This is accomplished by flexing the upper and lower limbs at the same time and maintaining the posture. There is no movement at all, so it is called internal exercise. The secret of the exercise is the relaxation of body and mind, so as to facilitate the flow of qi and blood. Although the person never moves, qi is rapidly generated, and the body feels hot and produces sweat all over, most profusely from the head, after 10 to 20 minutes. It is peculiar that the palms are warm and dry, although sweat glands are most densely distributed there, but vapour can be seen coming from the tips of the fingers, like cigarette smoke floating up.

Internal Qi

Qi in the form of electromagnetic force is, therefore, invisible and formless, but it can be felt. In practising Qigong, one can feel qi running along the channels in the body, and the heat it generates results in profuse sweating. The hands feel distended, numb, heavy, and warm due to increased blood flow under the influence of qi. The hands look red, from dilated blood vessels. One can feel the increased peristaltic movement of the stomach and intestines, and a lot of flatulence is released. Appetite is improved and constipation relieved. The mind becomes calmer, and insomnia disappears. It is only through Qigong exercise that we are able to get a glimpse of what qi is. A lot more of the mystery of qi is yet to be uncovered, and yet from the few pieces of this jigsaw puzzle, we are able to understand it more instead of regarding it as a trick on the mind. This is particularly important to acupuncturists who practise the art of regulating qi in the body and yet do not know how it works nor feel the effects of the treatment thoroughly. To them, the learning of Qigong not only gives them insight into the mechanism of qi, but also offers them another weapon in the fight against disease. I have discovered that a combination of external qi and acupuncture gives better results, especially in the treatment of inflammation and swelling, such as dental abscess, rhinitis, sinusitis, and conjunctivitis.

Functions of Qi

From accumulated knowledge and experience with Qigong and acupuncture, the function and properties of qi can be summarised as follows:

• **Life energy**

Qi is considered to be the source of life in Chinese medicine. It supplies energy to the various organs and to the tissues in the body for normal functioning. When qi is weak, sickness occurs, and if qi circulation is blocked, pain and swelling follow. When qi stops circulating, life comes to an end.

• **Maintaining blood flow**

Qi and blood always circulate together, the blood in the blood vessels and the qi in the fascia surrounding the blood vessels. Qi gives the driving force to the blood. As qi grows in strength through Qigong exercise, blood flow increases. This is particularly important in diseases caused by insufficient supply of blood, such as coronary insufficiency and arthritis.

• **Heat generation**

In the process of qi production, heat is generated by the muscles. Normal body temperature is maintained by the qi. When the qi is weak or qi circulation slows down, the body feels cold, especially at the extremities. This indicates that the health of the person is poor. In a seriously ill patient, if one holds the palm of the hand about 4–6 inches (10–15 cm) from the person's body, one can feel cold qi coming out of the patient, like a stream of cold air from an air conditioner. The sicker the patient is, the colder the qi. In my Qigong class, the most striking signs from patients after two to three weeks of daily exercise was that cold hands started to become warm and the cheeks appeared rosier.

Cold qi is called yin qi, and warm qi is called yang qi. During Qigong practice, yang qi gradually builds up. When someone has reached an advanced stage of Qigong exercise, he will not only feel warm; his yang qi is so strong that it will radiate from his body as heat to his surroundings.

• **Body resistance and defence against diseases**

Qi circulation in the superficial fascia together with the skin, called *wei qi* circulation, forms a defending shield to protect the body from the invasion of bacteria, virus, and other harmful elements. The skin serves as a mechanical barrier to invasion by micro-organisms, aided by the fatty acids and other substances found on the skin, which have potent antibacterial and antiviral properties and deter attack by harmful organisms. The qi in the superficial fascia protects the body from environmental changes and elements, such as extremes of heat, dampness, dryness, and cold, which enter the channels and cause imbalances in qi circulation, resulting in sickness. Qi also increases the production of interferon and T cells in the blood, which combat bacteria and viruses.

• **Homeostasis**

A tendency to uniformity or stability in the organism is essential for the survival of human beings and for maintaining normal health. Qi is the main force that keeps the body in this stable state. Qi circulation links the organs in the body. Qi flows between the organs, alternating from yin channel to yang channel and from yang channel to yin channel. It changes its polarity between different grades of yin and yang to strengthen the flow and to keep the various organs at their most efficient.

Qi controls the blood flow so that blood does not ooze out of the blood vessels. It also controls sweat and urine excretion, maintaining water concentration in the body. It controls the hormones and keeps them in balance, and prevents overflow of spermatozoa.

• **Promoting metabolism**

Qi serves as an impulse to start the biochemical transformation of food, enzymes, and hormones in the body. Through the metabolic process, food is broken down by enzymes to become nutrition and release electrical energy. Qi also promotes the conversion of nutrition to form enzymes and hormones in the body.

• **Anaesthesia and analgesia**

From 1958 to 1972, there were an estimated 600,000 cases of surgical operations in China making use of acupuncture anaesthesia. Qigong anaesthesia is a relatively new method of using external qi to induce a state of insensibility to pain, usually for operative purposes. It has no side effects and is not harmful. It is most suitable for patients who are not good candidates for drug-induced anaesthesia.

Thirty-four cases of thyroid gland operations using external qi emission were carried out in China between 1985 and 1989. All were conducted by the Qigong Master Mr Lim Hou Shen. All 34 cases were successful. External qi was directed either to Yintang extra point 1 (or Yintang Ex1), between the eyebrows, or Laogong P8 point, in the palm. The induction time was two to five minutes. The treating fingers and the palm were at a distance of about one foot (30 cm).

One of the main functions of external qi is to relieve pain. It has been found that after Qigong treatment, the pain threshold is generally raised. The analgesic effect is not only confined to the area receiving external qi, but is also extended to other parts of the body. A series of studies has been done in China on the treatment of cancer patients. The treating palm was placed about $1^1/_2$ feet ($^1/_2$ m) from the part to be treated. It took about three minutes to produce an analgesic effect. I have personally used external qi to treat cases of headache, toothache, and joint pain. The results were quite satisfactory.

Qi has been found to promote production of endorphins in the brain. The properties of endorphins are analogous to morphine in its analgesic effect.

Acupuncture and Qigong are used to build up qi for such purposes. This subject was a hot topic in the 1970s after former US President Nixon witnessed an anaesthetic procedure being done with acupuncture in China. The enthusiasm at the time was so focused on this particular aspect of analgesia that other therapeutic effects of qi were totally overlooked.

• Sedation

Qi can produce sedative effects due to its suppressive power on emotional disturbances and other irritating factors that can cause the neurons of the brain to become chaotic. It helps the cortex of the brain to rest and recover.

The first beneficial effect a person may feel after Qigong exercise is its calming effect. He will feel more relaxed, find it easier to fall asleep, and become less easily fatigued or irritated. Studies have been carried out in China on the treatment of schizophrenic patients using qi. After five minutes of treatment with external qi, the patient was known to fall asleep in his chair.

Qigong exercise can produce a sedative effect. When people practise Qigong, they feel very relaxed. For patients suffering from migraine or chronic fatigue syndrome, the first beneficial effect experienced is the disappearance of insomnia.

• Anti-inflammatory effect

Qi is composed partially of infrared radiation, which has anti-inflammatory properties, a fact well known in modern medicine. Infrared lamps are used for their anti-inflammatory action in physiotherapy in many hospitals and clinics. Qi, however, possesses more potent anti-inflammatory properties, as it also contains electromagnetic radiation. This anti-inflammatory effect can be acquired from:

- Qigong exercise as a self-treatment for chronic inflammatory masses in the body.
- External qi given to a patient to treat the inflammation.
- A combination of external qi with acupuncture, especially for acute cases of inflammation. This combined treatment is by far the most successful. I have treated quite a number of cases of dental abscess, purulent sinusitis, conjunctivitis, erythema multiforme, and Stephen-Johnson syndrome, particularly involving the mouth, with very dramatic results.

External Qi

Qi is produced by blood flow and muscle contraction in Qigong exercise. The process is analogous to running a car engine, which produces electricity that is stored in the battery. The human storage of qi is in the diaphragm and mesentery. This storage is different from that of a battery in that it cannot become overcharged because our body systems can adjust the qi so formed. When the level of qi is strong enough, it can be sent out of the body through the channels and acupuncture points to another person. This is external qi. It possesses the same properties as internal qi.

External Qi Used to Treat Sickness

Acupuncture points and channels are the receptors of qi and the orifice and passage for internal qi to be sent out from the body as external qi. External qi should be focused on acupuncture points, from which it can penetrate the patient's body and follow the channel network to produce the desired effect.

When external qi is given to a patient, the Laogong P8 point at the centre of the palm is normally used. The emitting palm is placed about 4–6 inches (10–15 cm) away from the acupuncture point. If the palm is placed over the forehead, the patient can feel the qi flowing down to the soles of his feet as numbness or warmth. If it is placed above the hand, a stream of warmth or numbness can be felt creeping up the forearm. When it reaches the upper arm, the patient's whole arm may be pulled up by the qi to float in the air. The patient will feel very relaxed and drowsy, warm and sweaty. By placing the palm over the temporal region of the head, headaches due to tension or migraine can be relieved, drunkards can be made to

EXTERNAL QI USED TO TREAT RHINITIS AND HEADACHE

After a minimum of two years of Qigong practice, you should be able to use external qi to treat mild complaints such as rhinitis or headache. Place your left palm 6 inches (15 cm) from Baihui G20 on the top of the head, and the right palm 6 inches (15 cm) from Yintang point between the eyebrows. Hold for 10 minutes. Complete the process by removing your left hand and bringing your right hand down along the nose to the chest and abdomen. The blocked nose will be relieved and the headache gone.

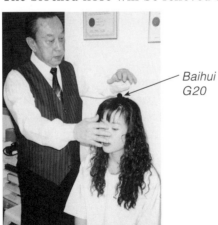

Baihui G20

Yintang Ex1

To treat dizziness and headache, place your palms 5 inches (13 cm) from the temporal lobes and hold 5 minutes. Complete the procedure by bringing your hands down along the neck and shoulders, drawing them down the arms and out from the fingertips. Repeat if necessary.

stop vomiting and become sober again, and giddiness can be reduced. If the palm is placed over a dental abscess, pain and swelling are relieved, and if placed over the nose, rhinitis or blocked nose will disappear. These are only a few examples of the treatment of sicknesses using external qi. The treating palm should be placed over the relevant acupuncture points for 20 to 30 minutes. The relief is immediate.

After constant daily practice for a year, every student of Kong Jing Qigong should be able to emit external qi from his palm at Laogong P8 point. But I would strongly advise that students do not give out qi to anyone, especially those students who have taken up Kong Jing Qigong in order to treat their own sickness. For the first two years, the exercise is mainly for building up qi, making it strong enough to regulate and readjust the qi in various organs and systems to produce a curing effect. The student may feel very fit, but he does not have enough qi to spare for others.

The past two hundred years have witnessed great advancements in various branches of science. However, when compared with atomic and space science, medical science is still a long way behind. The human race has been in existence on this earth for millions of years, and yet our knowledge of the human body is still in its infancy. Our minds and emotions, although we have located their site in the hypothalamus of the brain, are a mystery to us. For example, why does a person who is physically fit choose to be insane? We are still groping our way in the knowledge of body resistance and the immune system. Every time a new disease is discovered, we are at a loss. Even in the case of delayed pain sensations due to inflammation or ischaemia, western scientists have postulated that it may be due to muscular activity that releases a biochemical pain-producing factor which passes out into the tissue spaces and accumulates there, giving rise to pain. In Chinese medicine, this delayed pain is due to the blockage of energy, such that the qi and pain will disappear only if the obstruction is cleared.

Properties of External Qi

The existence of qi in the human body and the therapeutic effects of acupuncture and Qigong are beyond doubt. What we are looking for is how qi works and the true character of qi. The western world was interested in qi and its application and carried out scientific studies in this field long before the Chinese did. It is only in the past 20 to 30 years that the Chinese have done their own scientific studies on this subject. Many studies have been performed with Qigong masters on external qi and its properties, the results of which can be summarised thus:

• Radiation

External qi consists of an electromagnetic force that can radiate through space. A Qigong master can therefore transmit external qi to several persons at the same time. In May 1978 in Shanghai, China, a group of scientists worked with a few Qigong masters and found that the palms of the master could transmit a low-rate infrared electromagnetic wave. The same electromagnetic code could be detected in the patient at the same time, proving that external qi could be transmitted and received by another person. In one second, this low-rate wave gave a few up and down surges. At about 20-second intervals, there was a big surge. This low-rate frequency change of wave is similar to the sound waves of sea waves hitting rocks, and also similar to the sound waves produced by a mother humming her baby to sleep. The common feature of these codes is their ability to make people feel relaxed and calm and to get rid of fatigue.

Everyone in normal health is able to emit external qi, but the intensity is very weak. If their external qi is recorded using instruments, it will be seen as a straight line compared with those recorded from Qigong masters, which appear as wavy lines. The intensity of external qi can also be controlled by will.

• Magnetic

Qi is an electromagnetic energy and possesses positive and negative charges. The different poles become attracted to each other to form a circuit.

In a television program in Shanghai, China, in February 1985, Master Huang Jen Jong was seen to send out external qi to compasses on a table. He was able to disturb the needles of the compasses and make them rotate at will. The electromagnetic field he created thus must be greater than the earth's magnetic field to create such turmoil.

• Penetrating

External qi can penetrate walls, wood, and the human body. In an experiment done in China, Master Huang demonstrated that he could transmit qi through a lead sheet to a hemiplegic patient and control the movement of the paralysed limb. The penetrating power of external qi is therefore stronger than X-rays, which cannot penetrate lead.

• Transmissible

External qi can be transmitted to a person, and from him to another person.

• Delayed action

Although qi is composed of electromagnetic waves with the speed of light, when external qi is sent to another person, the reaction takes some time to occur, while the force slowly builds up.

• Storing

External qi can be sent out and stored in a person for a certain time, to be used later on. If the qi given to him is from a Qigong master, he can use it to treat another patient provided he is in normal health himself.

• Focusing

External qi from a student of Qigong spreads out in a fanlike radiation. It can be trained such that the qi comes out of the body in a spiral or is sent out from the hand in a beam to increase its penetrating power.

• Controllable

External qi can be controlled by the will. It can be emitted from the body by opening the palm and stopped by closing the hand into a fist. The power of qi can be increased by focusing the mind on the part of the body where the qi is to be sent.

Western medical philosophy is different from Chinese medical discipline. Western medicine tends to be more specific, being restricted to an individual organ or system. The electricity produced in the brain and the heart was discovered separately, and instruments were invented to record the electric energy and produce tracings—electroencephalograms from the brain and electrocardiograms from the heart. Sicknesses of these two organs are dealt with individually.

Chinese medicine is more general and is based on the belief that all organs in the body are linked by the qi circulating system, which exerts an influence on each separate organ. Through this connection, individual organs can also affect each other. Chinese medicine therefore places great emphasis on qi regulation through herbs, acupuncture, and Qigong to achieve therapeutic effects on sickness, treating the whole organism as a single entity.

It is only in the past 30 years that interest in this ancient Chinese art of healing has been rekindled. Modern scientific studies have been carried out to enhance our understanding of qi. It is an adventure that truly deserves our attention, as it will reveal yet another system in our body that is beyond the reach of western medicine. With more knowledge of this system, it may advance our understanding of our own body and help us to combat diseases with better weapons in the future.

Chapter 3

Qigong and the Polarity of Qi

"The yin and the yang are contained within the qi; the basic principle of the entire universe. They create all matter and its mutation. The qi is the beginning and the end, life and death."

—Huang Emperor, *Classic of Internal Medicine*

Qi means energy. Chinese scholars and physicians in the prehistorical period believed the universe and everything inside it was made of qi, which possessed yin and yang polarities. Prose on this yin-yang polarity, believed to go back as far as 1250 B.C., were eventually compiled in the *I Ching*, or the *Classic of Changes*. This book postulated the law of changes, which was further classified into 1) change, 2) exchange, and 3) unchange. Many branches of science have applied this theory to their research. The commercial world uses it in management; it was used in war to determine fighting strategies; mathematicians use it to perfect their calculations. It is also used in the computer sciences, and Chinese medicine makes use of it in the prevention and treatment of disease.

Polarity is the main principle of yin and yang. Qi possesses polarity with positive and negative poles, or yang and yin energy, similar to the two poles of a magnet or the positive and negative charges of electrical current. It applies to every process and phenomenon in the universe, from the cosmos to individual human beings. It explains the mystery of the transformation of movement and force. Like charges repel each other. Opposite charges attract each other. With the dynamic tension established by the polarity field, polarity can provide boundless forces to make the world go round, the earth rotate round the sun, electrical current run the engine, energy transform into essence and form, and to create life and death. It also demonstrates that all changes in the universe are cyclic rather than linear and therefore predictable.

The Principles of Yin and Yang

The principles of yin and yang can be summarized as follows:

• Opposite and unified

Yin and yang are opposite to each other and exist as one. In nature, all matter and phenomena exist in opposite phases—up and down, right and left, active and passive, hot and cold, day and night, summer and winter, happiness and sadness, male and female. They are opposites, yet they are related and exist as one.

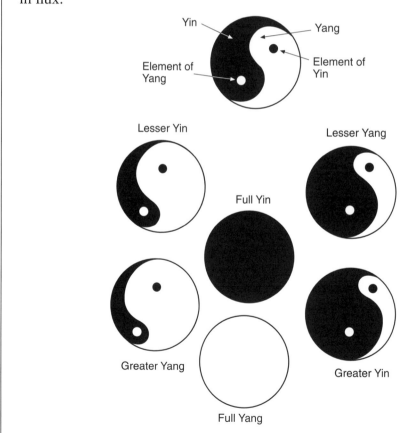

TAIJI SYMBOL

The Taiji symbol is often used to illustrate changes in the balance between yin and yang. The S-shaped boundary indicates that yin and yang are always in flux.

• Mutually dependent and interactive

Yin and yang cannot exist alone. They are not two different types of energy but rather two complementary phases of the same basic energy, like positive and negative electric charges. It takes two opposing charges to produce electric current or an electromagnetic field. If there is no top (yang), there will be no bottom (yin). If there is no male but only female, the species will perish.

• Mutually regulating

Yin and yang are mutually regulating, tending to a state of balance. The yang transforms and the yin conserves. In Chinese medicine, inside the yang qi there are some yin elements, and inside the yin qi there is also some yang energy. When yang qi has grown to its maximum degree and is resting, yin qi will start to grow and reduce the yang domination, and vice versa. The two states are never absolute or static; they are circulating and transforming all the time, seeking their complementary opposite in order to find the most stable balance.

This can be illustrated in the Taiji yin-yang circle, which represents the supreme source of half yin and half yang, each with a dot of its own opposite pole growing inside. The S-shape boundary between the two indicates that the two are flexible and never fixed. Whenever the waxing and waning of the polar energy leads to a critical excess of one or the other, it spontaneously transmutes into its own opposite to reestablish the balance. In nature, this can be seen in the formation of wind due to the regulating process of extreme differences of the atmospheric air pressure. In extreme cases, a cyclone occurs. The same is seen when the electric charges of the clouds and those of the Earth become excessive. The excessive charge of one will jump through the air to the opposite charge to produce lightning, thus reestablishing a balance. In human beings, when someone gets a fever (yang qi), the body breaks out in a sweat (yin), which carries excess heat out of the body and reestablishes a new equilibrium.

• Interchangeable

Yin and yang are interchangeable. In certain conditions, yin and yang can be changed entirely to the opposite phase. In the human body, this can be seen in muscle fibres, in which the negative charge inside is changed to positive and the positive charge outside the fibre is changed to negative, thus producing a flow of electricity. The same is seen in the circulation of qi in the human body, in which six channels are dominantly yang and the other six are dominantly yin. The 12 channels form a closed circuit. Qi flowing in the circuit changes its polarity alternately from yin to yang and from yang to yin as it goes from channel to channel. It is this interchange of yin and yang that gives the driving force for the qi to flow through all the channels smoothly and forcefully.

• Relativity

Yin and yang provide the measure to determine values and quality. These values are relative rather than absolute. Hot (yang) has no heat without cold (yin) to compare it with. Movement (yang) is not apparent if there is no stillness (yin) to measure it against. Light (yang) has no intensity of brightness if there is no darkness (yin) to serve as a standard of measurement. Good has no significant quality if there is no evil to show its value.

How Energy in the Cosmos Affects Human Beings

In the *Classic of Internal Medicine* it is written that the human being is an integral part of the universe, which consists of Heaven (with the stars, the sun, and the planets) as the yang pole and Earth as the yin pole. Thus we obey the polarity of the cosmos and follow its rhythm and force. In health and medical science, the law of yin and yang has many practical applications. The universe (as cosmos) and the human being are in similar resonance and energy equilibrium, and reflect each other. Every person has his own electromagnetic field, with the positive pole on the head and the negative pole in the sacrum. The individual's magnetic field interacts with the cosmic electromagnetic field and receives celestial energy from the sky through heat, while earth energy enters through the yin confluent part of the perineum. This energy circulates within the human energy circuit along the 12 channels of the qi system.

It is through this parallel convergence of the electromagnetic field of the earth with that of man that Qigong exercise attempts to build up qi within the body in resonance with the earth's magnetic field. It is also in this way that elemental environmental energies, such as the weather, cyclic changes of season, solar and lunar phases, and other external energies, find their entry to the human body, directly affecting the human energy system. Our body is thus tuned to follow the polarity changes of the cosmos. Every day starts with new yang after midnight and continues to full yang at noon. In the afternoon it starts with new yin, reaching full yin at midnight. We feel fresh and energetic with the yang energy in the morning, and become drowsy toward evening as our yang energy becomes worn out. Our heartbeats become less forceful, our breathing gets shallow, and our digestive system functions at a lower level as our brain, which controls all this, slows down with the diminishing yang energy.

Each month finds the yang energy rising from the new moon to the full moon, then the yin rising from the full moon to the new moon. The year also shifts rhythmically between yin and yang, with the new yang energy in spring increasing to full yang in summer. New yin starts in autumn, reaching full yin in winter.

From birth our body, with the control of the cosmos, sets up a biological rhythm, and life starts with the continuity between ourselves and our environment. We maintain good health by following the changes that surround us and adjusting our body energy in balanced and harmonious circulation. Abrupt changes in the lunar or seasonal energy pattern may affect us abnormally and put our energy out of balance. On the other hand, if our own energy system is not stable, the normal change of seasons or the lunar phases can upset the unstable energy system of our

THE EFFECTS OF EXTERNAL QI

Qi from the cosmos and from the earth's magnetic field interacts with the human electromagnetic field. Each person has his own electromagnetic field, with the positive pole at the head and the negative pole at the perineum. Positively charged cosmic energy enters through the head, while negatively charged energy from the earth's magnetic field enters through the perineum.

Scientific research has established that disturbances in the earth's magnetic field and microwave radiation affect our health. The earth's magnetic field can be disturbed by magnetic storms caused by solar flares, earthquakes, and volcanic eruptions. These disturbances in turn cause disturbances in our health. In addition, artificial electromagnetic fields produced by electrical power lines may be 30 times higher than levels determined to cause cancer growth and brain damage.

Studies have shown that power lines and microwave radiation primarily affect two types of tissue: brain tissue and rapidly developing tissues, such as those of foetuses, young children, cancerous tumours, and blood. Electromagnetic fields caused by computers, televisions, electric blankets, electric stoves, and cellular telephones have been linked to an increased risk of leukaemia, Down's syndrome, and cancer. Qigong is able to restore a disturbed electromagnetic field to the normal range (7–10 Hz), thus restoring normal health.

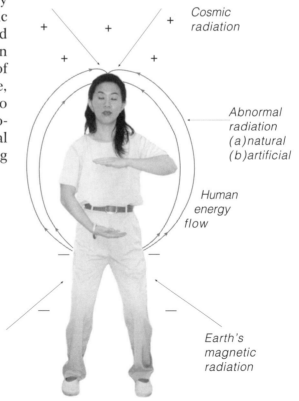

Cosmic radiation

Abnormal radiation
(a)natural
(b)artificial

Human energy flow

Earth's magnetic radiation

body and cause it to become chaotic. The best example can be seen in the psychiatric patient who becomes uncontrollable on full moon nights when the new yin energy is beginning to rise from the full yang.

Polarity in the Organs

The polarity of yin-yang energy plays an important role in our health. The proper functioning of the organs in the body is a prerequisite to normal health.

Each organ in the body is designated as yin or yang according to its form and function. Yin is regarded as solid and is associated with form. It involves the solid organs, such as the heart, liver, kidneys, spleen, and lungs. Yang is hollow and is related to function. Yang involves organs such as the large intestine, stomach, small intestine, urinary bladder, pleural and peritoneal cavities, and gall bladder. The organs are paired according to similarity in energy function and physiological function. Energy function pairings are seen in the lung and large intestine channels, heart and small intestine channels, and spleen and stomach channels. Those based on physiological functions are seen in the pairing of the kidney and bladder channels. This coupling of the channels is important in the regulation of qi to produce therapeutic results. The adjustment of yin and yang energy in one channel can also give a therapeutic effect to the partner of the channel.

greater yin	Lungs	Large intestine	bright yang
greater yin	Spleen	Stomach	bright yang
lesser yin	Heart	Small intestine	greater yang
lesser yin	Kidneys	Bladder	greater yang
absolute yin	Pericardium	Triple Warmer (Sanjiao)	lesser yang
absolute yin	Liver	Gall bladder	lesser yang

The Chinese therapeutic approach is unique in its emphasis on homeostasis and harmonious balance of the energy system in the body. To the Chinese, the correction of an imbalance of yin-yang energy in a sick organ will cure the disease. The maintenance of an optimum yin-yang equilibrium is the key to health.

Yin and Yang Energy Change in the Life Process

Qi possesses polarity and is flowing matter. The movement of matter follows certain rules. Movement starts in an upward and outward direction, followed by a downward and inward motion. Through mutual transmutation, it gives rise to numerous changes.

Yin and yang and the direction of their movements are terms used to explain characteristic changes of the specific function of matter. If we call the form of matter yin and the energy of matter yang, the rising and outgoing motion as yang and the falling and inward movement as yin, then, when the energy of the matter increases to an extent that is greater than the weight of the matter, this energy (yang) will pull matter (yin) upward. This is called carrying the yin upward. When the energy (yang) has been consumed to less than its body weight, the matter will maintain its own energy (yin) and fall downward. This is known as bringing the yang down. The upward and downward movement in a circle is known as Taiji. The yin and yang way of motion is called the poles of Taiji.

In order to study the change of function and the different characteristics of transmutation, it is convenient to further divide the rising and falling yin and yang energy into upper and lower parts, each according to its energy capacity. The upper portion of the yang energy, which rises as a result of its greater energy, is called greater yang. The lower portion of the rising part contains less energy and is called lesser yang. The upper portion of the descending part, which possesses more energy than the lower portion, is called lesser yin. The lower portion, which has very little energy and thus descends faster and lower, is termed greater yin. If we use the sign (—) for yang energy and (– –) for yin, we can illustrate the different characteristics of qi and its function very clearly in a comprehensive diagram. The great yang can be represented by (⚌), lesser yang as (⚎), great yin as (⚏), and lesser yin by (⚍). Thus one yang and one yin are divided into four and they can be further divided into smaller portions to represent the different grades of energy change. This is used in the classification of the 12 main channels of the body.

The same sign can also be used to illustrate the energy change in a person from birth until death. From the lifeless state of complete yin (☷) to the formation of the embryo, life starts with the addition of one portion of yang from below (☶). From here the life force increases gradually, to half yin on top and half yang at the bottom (☳), and finally to complete yang (☰). From this pinnacle of complete yang, the yang energy begins to dwindle through sickness, excessive sexual activity, and environmental pollution. The yin portion is increased continuously until it reaches half yang at the top and half yin added from below (☴). The bioenergy continues to wear off until it comes to a completely yin state without yang qi (☷), indicating the end of life.

This combination of yin and yang symbols is called the Pahquer sign. This is a simple way to illustrate energy changes, the ratio of yin and yang at each state, and the characteristics of energy change from stage to stage. Kuen (☷), the extreme yin state, indicates that there is total absence of energy, like the silent Earth. Tay (☷☰) shows three yin on the top with three yang below: yin energy is descending and yang energy is rising. The two energies intermingle, interacting and making use of each other such that a balanced state is obtained, neither too hot (yang) nor too cold (yin). Therefore, the qi at this stage is smooth, freely flowing. Chien (☰) is complete yang. The energy has developed to its utmost and is able to utilise the full capacity of its energy force, like the big sky. Foou (☰☷), with its top three yang and lower three yin, is not a good qi. The yang energy is rising and the yin descending. The two energies are dislocated and unable to interact. The rising heat has nothing to cool it off, and the descending cold (yin) has nothing to warm it up. The energy at this stage therefore wears off very rapidly.

If we apply this change of energy to the life process of a person, taking the whole life span to be 80 years, then 20 years of age is the starting point of the Tay stage, which is the golden age of a person. The qi channels are flowing freely and the energy is plentiful; the mind is alert, and the person is most productive sexually. This state continues until it reaches the Chien stage.

Forty years is the beginning of the Foou stage, where mind and physical stamina start to slow down. Degeneration of the organs starts to wear them down. Qi dwindles gradually from 40 to 60 years. The yin and yang are dislodged. Qi circulation starts to become obstructed, and the person finds himself a frequent visitor to medical clinics and hospitals, with diseases such as hypertension, heart attack, stroke, and diabetes, the common associates of old age. This is a natural process of life that no one is able to escape.

THE LIFE PROCESS

In the natural life process, life starts from a lifeless state indicated by (☷) to the formation of an embryo, indicated by the addition of one portion of yang qi from below (☷). From here it continues through the growing period, with the gradual addition of yang qi until it reaches full yang (☰), the peak of life. From this point, aging starts to set in, shown by a loss of yang qi from below and the addition of yin qi to take its place (☲). This process goes on until it reaches a state of complete loss of yang (☷), at which point life comes to an end.

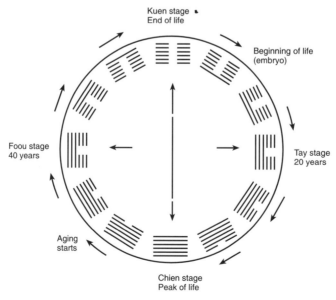

QIGONG AND THE LIFE PROCESS

The purpose of Qigong is to build up qi to reverse the aging process, leading from the Foou stage (☰) back to the youthful Tay stage (☷). In doing this, we are not reversing the cycle from Foou through Chien back to Tay, as no one can challenge life itself. Instead, Qigong attempts to take a shortcut from the Foou stage across to the Tay stage, thus delaying the aging process.

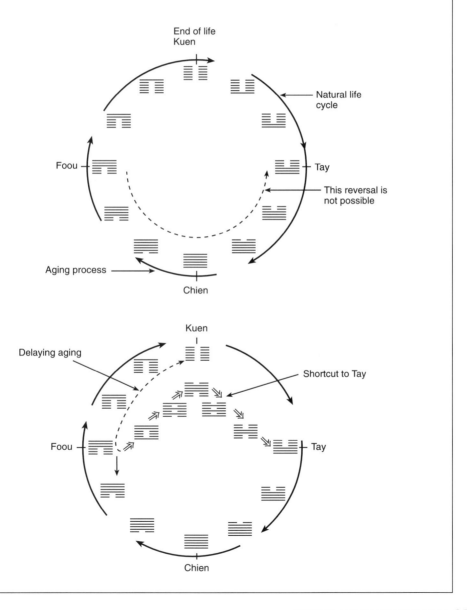

However, ancient Chinese physicians believed that although we could not challenge fate, if we were prepared for this danger and changed our lifestyle, we could prevent sickness or the process of degeneration. If we took positive steps in strengthening the body with Qigong or other physical exercises, we could not only build our health, but would even rejuvenate our bodies, and we would thus live a longer life.

Emotions and Polarity

The cerebrum, the most developed portion of the brain, is the centre of emotion. Excitation of the cerebrum is expressed in emotional activity as anger, joy, worry, sadness, fear, apprehension, or perturbation. The emotions are closely related to yin-yang polarity. Mild emotional stimulation releases only moderate amounts of energy changes of yin and yang. Our body systems are able to adjust to this change. When we are angry, creating a strong yang energy phase, our body reacts in short, fast breathing with strong expiration to get rid of the extra yang energy. According to the Chinese theory of the five elements, emotion is closely associated with the organs of the body. Anger is related to the liver, joy and shock to the heart, fear to the kidneys, sadness to the lungs, and worry to the spleen. Extreme emotional disturbances can unleash very strong yin and yang charges beyond the coping ability of our body systems, resulting in pathological changes. We often come across cases of extreme anger that give rise to a sudden excess of yang energy in the head, causing malignant hypertension, and ending up with a cerebrovascular accident and death. Extreme joy and shock usually occur when a person suddenly receives unexpected good or bad news. The excessive yang energy rushes suddenly to the heart, causing arrhythmia and stopping the heart.

Yin and Yang Polarity and Qigong

The balance of yin and yang energy is the cornerstone of all the different schools of Qigong exercise. Qigong exercise applies the principle of yin and yang, dividing the body into different areas of yin and yang controlled by the principle of polarity. Thus the back, external, and upper parts of the body, including the head, are yang. The perineum, the front, internal and lower parts of the body are yin. The solid organs, including the lungs, spleen, heart, liver, and kidneys, are yin. The hollow organs, like the large intestine, stomach, small intestine, urinary bladder, and gall bladder, are yang. Movement of the body is yang and stillness is yin. The kidney is yin and the heart is yang.

The application of the yin-yang principle to Qigong exercise can be seen in various situations.

• Posture

This is important in building up qi through contraction of the muscles and by strengthening qi circulation through a feedback method. The yin-yang principle of balance between two opposing poles provides the basis for Qigong postures designed to bring about harmony of energy through interaction and transmutation.

THE FIVE ANIMALS QIGONG

This earliest known Qigong exercise was formulated by the famous surgeon Hua Tuo between A.D. 160 and 190. Its characteristic features are meditation and mind control of qi circulation. (In this aspect it differs from Kong Jing Qigong, where the mind is not allowed to interfere with qi.) The Five Animals Qigong is done in standing, sitting or lying posture with hands at the sides. The body and mind are relaxed with meditation. The stillness of the body reaches a stage when it starts to change to involuntary activity such as crying, laughing, or movements simulating the five animals—tiger, bear, deer, eagle, and monkey—associated with the five elements and organs.

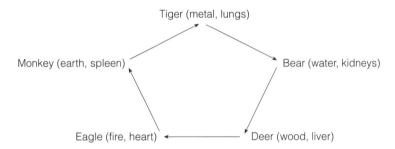

Metal begets water, water begets wood, wood begets fire, fire begets earth, and earth begets metal. The movements usually start with those of the tiger, then change to those of a bear, a deer, an eagle, and a monkey, in that order. If the movements of a certain animal are prolonged, it indicates that the associated organ is sick. When the movements have passed through the stages in the correct sequence, the body soon reaches a more advanced stage of qi. It then changes from activity to stillness again—the body is on its way to good health, and the disease is cured.

THE INTERNAL AND EXTERNAL ELIXIRS

Elixir, in Chinese, is Dan Tien. It is where qi is stored in the abdomen, in the diaphragm and under the umbilicus. Since the time of Da Mol, Qigong exercise has been categorized into various degrees of internal and external forms called Nei Dan, or internal elixir, and Wai Dan, external elixir. The two elixirs are classified according to the degree of stillness and motion. At one end is internal elixir, which includes meditation and Qigong exercise, involving the building of qi and its regulation inside the body. At the other is the martial art that includes fighting techniques and strengthening of the hands and feet to break brick and stone with qi from the body.

In Qigong exercise, movement to the right must be followed by movement to the left, and an upward posture must be balanced with a downward posture in order to strike a balance in the yin and yang force.

Choice of posture is important in the treatment of sickness. Whether a posture is yin or yang is very important. In hypertension, for example, which brings a lot of yang energy to the head, it is better to do Qigong exercise in a yin posture, i.e. sitting down, or in the Horse Stance posture, lowering the forearms below horizontal to create more yin energy to counteract the excess yang energy and lower the blood pressure.

• Stillness and movement

Stillness is yin, and movement is yang. The appropriate movement and stillness greatly affect the yin-yang energy in the body. Qigong exercise makes use of movement to counter stillness, and stillness to start movement.

Qigong follows the law of yin-yang, which states that yang moves to its greatest extension and then rests, and yin rests to its extreme and then moves. One is constantly changing into the other to strike the most stable balance. This transmutation is able to regulate the function of the internal organs through the resulting qi circulation. This is seen sometimes in the internal elixir, the Five Animals Qigong, in which involuntary movements of the body begin after a certain period of stillness and meditation.

Qigong also uses movement of the arms and flexing of the fingers to lead the circulation of yin and yang qi in the channels. Kong Jing Qigong uses the flexing of individual fingers of both hands to regulate qi circulation in the channels controlled by the different fingers.

• Breathing in yin and yang regulation

Inhalation is yang, as we breathe in yang energy from the oxygen in the air. Exhalation is yin, when the unclean carbon dioxide gas is breathed out. A few schools of Qigong place great emphasis on breathing to regulate the yin-yang balance and increase breathing capacity by increased movement of the diaphragm, chest muscles, and abdominal muscles.

In normal conditions, when emotional agitation occurs, as in anger due to excess yang, the central nervous system corrects the imbalance by making the lungs increase exhalation to expel the excessive yang accumulated by anger. At the same time, inhalation is shortened to decrease the inflow of yang energy from the air, thereby reestablishing a balance of yin and yang energy in the body. Likewise with sadness, which is prominent in the yin phase, making one feel down and low. The qi swings to the yin phase of breathing, with deep inhalation to take in more yang energy from the air to counterbalance the excess yin.

• Yin and yang in association with mind control

The mind is the central control of the qi. During Qigong exercise in cold weather, the mind can imagine being in a warm room to stimulate yang qi in the body. In a hot climate one can think of the seaside with a cool breeze to harmonize qi circulation with yin qi. In getting yang qi from the cosmos, the mind focuses on the top of the head, at Baihui G20. As the person breathes, he imagines that the qi from the cosmos is coming through the Baihui with every inhalation. In getting rid of aberrant yin energy, with every exhalation the mind leads the qi in the body downward to the centre of the foot, at Yongquan K1.

• Time of Qigong practice

The time of practice refers to the hours of the day as well as seasons of the year. In temperate climates, spring and summer are the best seasons for building up yang qi, as the atmosphere is full of yang energy. The active type of Qigong, the external elixir, is most suitable. Autumn and winter are yin seasons. The less active form of Qigong, the internal elixir, is better.

Yin and yang energy in nature grows and fades, ceaselessly changing. The change of the four seasons, the new moon and the full noon, day and night are all reflections of the change of yin and yang. This rhythm of changes also occurs in the human body, which resonates with nature's rhythm. Ancient Chinese physicians made use of this fact to formulate the best time for Qigong practice. It was found that breathing exercise and Qigong exercise were best practised from midnight to noon, at the time when the yang qi was growing from new yang to full yang qi at noon. According to the theory of the internal elixir, the best time to practise Qigong is at midnight. The second choice is noon, and the third choice is 5–7 o'clock either in the morning or afternoon.

The main object of Qigong is to build up the life essence and to change this essence to energy. To do so, the water energy from the kidneys must be raised to meet the fire energy of the heart and reach a balance between these two original *yen qi* of the body. Yen qi is the original qi, which everyone is born with. The yen qi circulates in the body in a fixed pattern daily: midnight in the kidneys, 5–7 a.m. in the liver, noon in the heart, and 5–7 p.m. in the lungs. Therefore midnight, when the yang qi starts to become active in the kidneys, is the best time to do Qigong to bring the yang qi up to meet the fire energy in the heart.

In traditional Chinese medicine it is believed that the activity of yin and yang energy in the human body is synchronised with the change of yin and yang energy in nature. Midnight and the end of winter are when yin ends and new yang starts, coinciding with the growth of new yang in the human body at midnight. It is therefore the best time to practise Qigong to get the best results, in line with the principle of nature and the human body reacting synchronously. Noon is also a good time for Qigong practice, as it is the time of change from diminishing yang to the new yin. During the hours of 5–7 in the morning and afternoon, the kidneys and the heart, or water and fire energy, are in equilibrium. This is a good time for meditation and exercise, but not the best.

• Yin and yang in relation to the direction of practice

The up-and-down and top-and-bottom phases in the human body can be represented in two ways, either as empty on top and solid at the bottom (yang top yin bottom) or solid up and empty down (yin up and yang down). Chinese medicine makes use of this difference in vertical energy level to define various diseases. An extreme upward flow of yang qi can be seen in hypertension, headaches, and cerebrovascular accidents. An excessive downward flow of qi is seen in diabetes, prolapsed organs, and menorrhagia.

Qigong uses the mind to help regulate the vertical flow of qi and correct imbalances. In the case of excessive rising qi in hypertension, the mind is focused lightly at the Yongquan K1 point at the centre of the sole of the foot, thus leading the qi downward to leak out from the Yongquan point. In Kong Jing Qigong, this is done by bending the forearm slightly down from the horizontal while in the Horse Stance, or by flexing the wrist and bending both palms down from the vertical in the Embracing the Moon step, to push the qi down from the head.

In the *Classic of Changes* it is stated that the two poles, yin and yang, can develop into four phenomena that correlate to spring, summer, autumn, and winter, and to east, west, south, and north. The four directions are associated closely with the five elements—metal, water, wood, fire, and earth. The directions are also linked to the organs of the body. South is related to the heart and belongs to fire, west to the lungs and metal, north to the kidneys and water, east to liver and wood. The centre is associated with the spleen and earth.

To obtain good results from Qigong exercise, it is essential to get qi in the body to synchronise with the qi in nature. This is done by following the direction of the earth.

• Facing south

South is associated with the heart and fire, and north with the kidneys and water. Both are in alignment with the earth's yin and yang directions. When the person faces south, the front of the body, which is yin, takes in yang energy from the south. The back, which is yang, absorbs yin energy from the north. The kidneys and the heart interchange energies and build up a new balance of yin and yang qi to benefit the health of the body. Scientifically, by facing south the body is cutting across the earth's magnetic field from south to north, and will receive a great amount of energy from this magnetic field.

• Choosing a direction according to the organ and sickness

It is useful to face the direction that is associated with the sick organ. For example, a person with a disease of the liver or its connected organs (the eyes) and associated tissues (the muscles or the tendons) would be advised to face east when performing Qigong exercise for the best therapeutic effect.

• Gender and direction

A man who faces north during Qigong exercise will receive yin qi from that direction, which compensates for the male yang qi. A woman who faces south is able to receive yang qi to regulate the yin energy in her body.

• Time of day and direction

The time of day reflects the transformation of yin and yang in nature. When this effect is coupled with that produced by direction, the qi in the universe can influence the qi in the body, the microcosmos. The period from 5 to 7 in the morning is new yang, the spring of a day. The liver belongs to new yang of the yin energy, and its position is east. It is best to practise Qigong facing east between 5 and 7 a.m.

CORRELATIONS OF YIN AND YANG

Yin and yang polarity can be broken down into four elements (greater yin, lesser yin, greater yang, and lesser yang), which correlate with the compass directions, organs of the body, seasons of the year, the five elements, emotions, and times of day. Direction, for instance, can be utilized in maximizing the effect of Qigong practice.

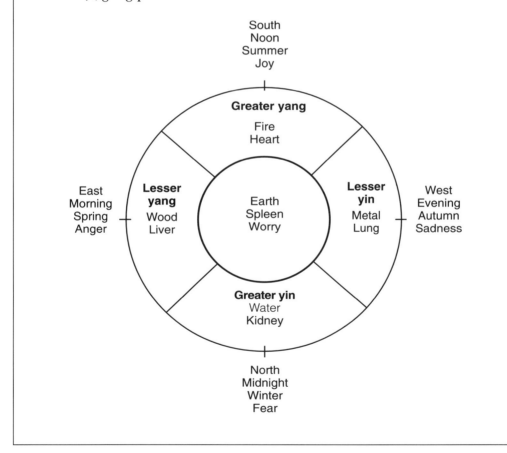

Noon is a time of greater yang and corresponds to summer and the southern direction. It is best to do Qigong exercise facing south at this hour. Between 5 and 7 p.m. is the autumn of the day with its position in the west. It is best to do Qigong exercise facing west at this time of day. At midnight, which is the time for the kidneys, it is the time of greater yin; facing north is best.

The choice of direction is based on the principle of synchronising nature and human qi. By choosing position and timing logically, you get the most out of nature's huge supply of energy, and obtain the best results from Qigong exercise.

THE CYCLES OF GENERATION AND DESTRUCTION

The Chinese classify everything in the universe into five elements: wood, fire, earth, metal, and water. These five elements are interrelated through generative and destructive cycles. The circle in this diagram represents the cycle of generation, in which worry begets sadness, which begets fear, which begets anger, and so on. Similarly, earth nourishes metal, which nourishes water, which nourishes wood, and so on.

The cycle of destruction is represented by the five-pointed star, in which worry destroys fear, fear destroys joy, joy destroys sadness, and so on. Similarly, metal is melted by fire, fire is controlled by water, and so on.

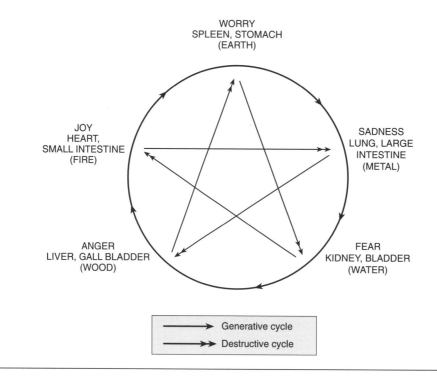

Chapter 4

Qigong and the Channels of Qi:
The Human Energy Network

Qi, or bioenergy, circulates in the human body following a definite, well-connected pathway in a closed circuit. This circuit was traced by Chinese physicians long ago. The energy network connects the inner organs for mutual adjustment through the circulation of qi, in order to create a stable internal environment favourable to the health of the body. It also connects the inner organs to the skin, through which communication with the outside world is established. This energy network is called jing luoh, the energy channels. Along each channel there are certain points that act as mirrors reflecting the condition of the inner organs. These points get very tender when the organ related to that particular channel is sick. At the same time, the points act as windows through which qi from within the body can come out and qi from outside can come in. These are called acupuncture points.

Interrelation of Organs

Chinese physicians consider that all organs are interconnected. The nose is linked to the lungs, the eyes to the liver, the ears to the kidneys, the tongue to the heart, and the mouth to the spleen and stomach. The sickness of one may be due to an unhealthy state in the other. For example, the eyes of a hepatitis B carrier often become inflamed, while unhealthy kidneys often lead to impaired hearing. There are also connections between internal organs. This takes the form of coupling. The lungs are linked to the large intestine, the stomach to the spleen, the heart to the small intestine, the bladder to the kidneys, the gall bladder to the liver, and the pericardium to the pleural or peritoneal cavity. The treatment of one organ through its qi channel often cures sickness in the other organ. For example, stimulation of an acupuncture point on the large intestine channel can also cure ailments of the lung. Therapeutic principles in Chinese medicine are based mainly on holistic treatment, that is, the treatment of whole body systems.

How the Qi Network was Established

Acupuncture and Qigong have been using the qi channels to treat sickness for several thousand years, and yet until today, its anatomical existence has not been verified. The scalpel and microscope have been used by quite a number of scientists to trace the course of the qi channels, but no one has yet been successful in locating them in the tissues of the body. X-rays have been used in recent years by groups of scientists in Taiwan and France. They were able to show the presence of acupuncture points and part of the course of the channels, but these have never been shown anatomically.

Let us look at how the ancient Chinese physicians were able to map out the 12 main channels and the eight extra meridians without the help of modern scientific instruments.

The first principle that they made use of was the physiological function of qi. As an energy, qi is not visible nor can it be measured in the same way as electricity, but it feels like an electric current that gives you a shock. The presence of qi can only be felt by those people who have been practising Qigong for a period of time. The main aim in Qigong exercise is to build up the amount of qi in the body. When the amount of qi is increased, the flow of the qi becomes very strong and the channels open up more. When a person has reached this stage of practice, which usually takes about two months, he will be able to feel the flow of qi under the skin like the creeping of an insect or the flow of a warm stream, with a sensation of itchiness, numbness, fullness, and warmth. This sensation is due to the flow of qi in the channels, and thus the path can be traced and marked.

Qi flows in the body vertically from the head to the extremities. With the aid of Qigong exercise and the sensation of the flow of qi on the skin, areas of individual channels can roughly be marked out running from the chest to the finger, from the finger to the head and continuing down to the foot, and from the foot to the chest organs in one round, forming four channels. Starting from the chest again, it continues in the same direction, which can also be traced out, in the second and third rounds to form another eight channels to complete the circle of 12 main channels in the body.

When sickness strikes the body, the pathological changes in the organs are reflected in a small area on the surface of the body. This presents itself as a tender spot. A group of these small areas can be singled out to reflect the different complaints from a particular organ. These spots can then be joined up in a line to represent the pathway of qi flow for that organ. This is called the channel of that organ, and the point is called the acupuncture point. The best illustration is seen in diseases of the heart. In modern medicine, when a heart attack occurs, a crushing pain is felt from the left upper chest coursing down the armpit along the medial side of the arm and forearm down to the tip of the little finger. This is exactly the same path that Chinese physicians had marked out thousands of years ago as the heart channel, a channel they used to diagnose and treat heart disease.

Sometimes acupuncture points are found to be near a pathological lesion. For instance, in herpes zoster (shingles) on the chest wall, the point is located near the spinal column, which modern medicine has identified as the location of the ganglion of the spinal nerve, exactly where the virus invades to cause the herpes.

Certain points are located on one organ channel but are used to treat sickness of other organs. These are found along the bladder channel at the back, on both sides of the spinal column. For example, the lung acupuncture point was found to be at the side of the third thoracic vertebra, the heart point at the side of the fifth thoracic vertebra, the kidney point at the side of the second lumbar vertebra—all $1^1/_2$ inches (3 cm) from the central line of the back. These points can be traced anatomically above the sympathetic nerve chain where the nerves branch out to supply the corresponding organs mentioned above.

Sometimes, a disease of one organ can present an associated clinical feature in another organ. This is seen, for example, in the redness and dryness in the eyes due to liver dysfunction. These interrelations between organ and organ, and between organ and channel were the pointers that Chinese physicians used to chart the various channels.

In a typical acupuncture treatment, a needle is put on a point of one channel and another needle is put at a point on another channel, for example one at the point Jianyu LI15 of the right large intestine channel on the right shoulder and another at the point Zu-Sanli S36 of the left stomach channel on the left leg. After stimulating the flow of qi in the channel with finger manipulation, external qi is sent into the body through the Jianyu LI15 point. The left leg would feel a strong flow of qi coming down from the right shoulder, raising the leg off the couch. This demonstration that the large intestine channel communicates directly with the stomach channel is one of the methods that ancient Chinese physicians used to connect all the 12 main channels in describing the closed circuit of qi flow.

The description of the energy channels in the paragraphs above is based mainly on bedside medical experience, Qigong, and acupuncture.

The Energy Channels System

The energy channels chart is a comprehensive tabulation. It is used mainly in acupuncture for the treatment of diseases. For the purposes of Qigong exercise, only the 12 main channels and a few of the extra meridians are involved. A brief introduction to these channels is essential for the understanding of Qigong exercise.

The 12 main channels are:

1. Hand greater yin lung channel: from the side of the upper chest to the lateral side of the arm and forearm down to the thumb.
2. Hand bright yang large intestine channel: from the tip of the index finger on the dorsum, or back, of the hand to the lateral side of the forearm, up the

arm to the shoulder, along the side of the neck to the face, ending at the side of the nose.

3. Foot bright yang stomach channel: from the head and face down the neck to the chest, the abdomen, and down the lateral side of the thigh and leg to end at the second toe.

4. Foot greater yin spleen channel: from the medial side of the big toe up the leg and thigh to the abdomen, finishing at the side of the chest to complete the first circle.

5. Hand lesser yin heart channel: from the armpit down the medial side of the arm and forearm to reach the palm, stopping at the tip of the little finger.

6. Hand greater yang small intestine channel: from the tip of the little finger along the medial side of the hand to the forearm and arm to the back of the shoulder and neck, ending on the side of the face.

7. Foot greater yang bladder channel: from the head down the occiput (back of the head) and neck to the back of the body to the buttocks, down the posterior of the lower limbs to the foot, ending at the lateral side of the fifth toe.

8. Foot lesser yin kidney channel: follows the bladder channel from the fifth toe upward along the sole and medial side of the foot to the leg and thigh, along the abdomen to the front of the chest to complete the second circle.

9. Hand absolute yin pericardium channel: from the chest down the middle of the arm and forearm to the middle of the palm, ending at the tip of the middle finger.

10. Hand lesser yin triple warmer (Sanjiao) channel: from the pericardium channel, it runs from the tip of the fourth finger along the back of the hand up the middle of the dorsal side of the forearm and arm, along the shoulder to the side of the face.

11. Foot lesser yang gall bladder channel: from the face it continues from the triple warmer (Sanjiao) down the side of the neck and body, along the lateral side of the thigh and leg, to end up at the tip of the fourth toe.

12. Foot absolute yin liver channel: from the big toe to the dorsum of the foot up the medial side of the leg and thigh to the chest to complete the third circle.

From the courses of the 12 channels, it is apparent that the flow of qi forms three cycles from hand to foot, making one closed circuit starting from the lung channel to the liver channel. When the circulation is finished, it starts again from the lung channel, making roughly 54 rounds in a day.

The energy channels run longitudinally, parallel to each other, from the head to the foot and hand, symmetrically on both sides of the body. They provide a close connection between the various tissues and the organs, joining them from left to right, up and down, communicating to the outside through the acupuncture points in a closed circuit. From the organs inside the body, they communicate along the channels with the five sense organs, the seven openings, and the four limbs, running throughout the body to provide a pathway for the circulation of qi that regulates the function of the organs, keeping them in perfect harmony and health.

The 12 main channels connect directly with the viscera, each organ with its own channel. Each channel is distributed with a number of acupuncture points that serve as windows and mirrors to the outside world. It is through these points that external qi from the body can be sent to another person and external aberrant energies, such as wind, heat, and coldness, can invade the body to cause disturbances in the qi circulation. It is a mirror because it can reflect the sickness inside the system as a tender spot on the skin.

The Naming of the Channels

The name of each channel is based on the limb where it starts or ends; its polarity, i.e., either yin or yang; and the name of the organ to which it is connected.

On the four limbs, the medial side close to the body is yin. The lateral side away from the body is yang. On the body trunk, the front is yin and the back is yang, except for the stomach, which is a yang organ.

The five solid organs (the lungs, spleen, heart, kidneys, and liver) are yin. The five hollow organs (the large intestine, stomach, small intestine, bladder, and gall bladder) are yang.

Transmutation of Energy

Qi circulation can be traced in the diagrams that follow, starting with the lung greater yin (taiyin) to large intestine bright yang (yangmin), stomach bright yang, spleen greater yin, heart lesser yin (shaoyin), small intestine greater yang (taiyang), bladder greater yang, kidney lesser yin, pericardium absolute yin (jueyin), triple warmer (Sanjiao) lesser yang (shaoyang), gall bladder lesser yang, liver absolute yin, and back to lung again. There is transmutation of the energy from yin to yang and back as it flows from one channel to the other. This is important in producing movement of the qi and increasing the strength of the flow, very much like alternating electric current.

The points where the transformation of the energy begins to take place are located at the wrist and below the ankle as follows: Taiyuan L9, Sanjian LI3, Taibai SP3, Shugu B65, Daling P7, Zu-Linqi GB41, Taichong Liv3, Shenmen H7, Xiangu S43, Houxi SI3, Taixi K3, Zhongzhu TW3.

These are important points for using acupuncture to regulate the energy in the two channels on either side of the point, as at these points it is easiest to change between yin and yang energy. Kong Jing Qigong makes full use of these areas to adjust the flow of qi and to influence the change of energy. This is done by flexing a finger and letting the tension of the flexed muscles and tendons stimulate the acupuncture points.

The fact that the qi circuit starts with the lung channel has dual significance. It is through the lungs that a baby gets its first breath of life. It is also the lungs (with their respiratory and expiratory movement) that provide the driving force for the circulation of qi throughout the body.

THE LUNG CHANNEL OF TAIYIN

The lung channel originates in the abdomen at Zhongwan C12 point and runs down to connect with the large intestine. Turning back, it follows the cardiac orifice and passes through the diaphragm to enter the lungs, continuing up to the throat. It then runs across to the shoulder, where it emerges at its first point and then descends along the medial side of the upper arm to reach the anterior border of the radius bone on the medial side of the forearm to pass Yuji point, terminating at the tip of the thumb. The branch at the wrist splits from Lieque L7 and runs directly to the radial side of the tip of the index finger, connecting the large intestine channel.

There are 11 points along the course. Acupuncture applied at these points can treat diseases of the lungs and throat and any pain along the channel. Commonly used points are Yuji L10, Taiyuan L9, and Lieque L7.

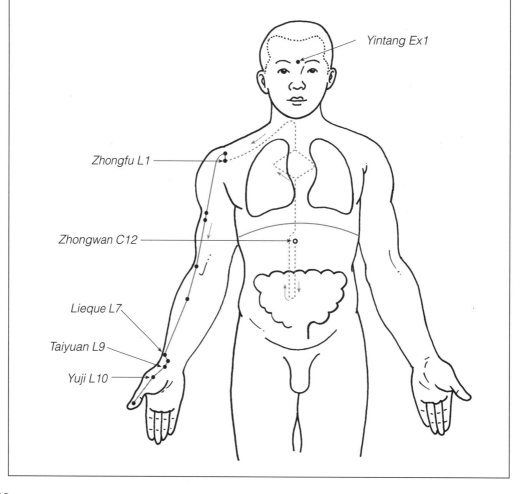

Yintang Ex1

Zhongfu L1

Zhongwan C12

Lieque L7

Taiyuan L9

Yuji L10

THE LARGE INTESTINE OF HAND YANGMIN CHANNEL

The large intestine channel originates at the tip of the index finger and runs upward along its lateral side, passing the space between the thumb and index finger, where Hegu LI4 is located. The channel continues upward to reach the lateral aspect of the elbow, where Quchi LI11 is situated. From there it goes to the lateral side of the shoulder to Jianyu LI15, and turns to the back of the seventh cervical vertebra and then forward to the supra-clavicular fossa. At this point the channel divides into two branches. The first branch passes through the lungs and diaphragm to reach the large intestine. The second branch ascends along the neck to the cheek and crosses below the nose to Yingsiang LI20, connecting with the stomach channel at Chengqi S1.

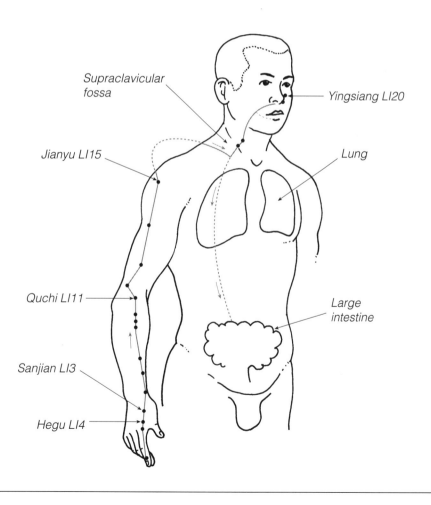

Supraclavicular fossa

Yingsiang LI20

Jianyu LI15

Lung

Quchi LI11

Large intestine

Sanjian LI3

Hegu LI4

THE STOMACH CHANNEL OF FOOT YANGMIN

The stomach channel starts at Chengqi S1 at the root of the nose, below the eye, and descends to the corner of the mouth. It turns back along the lower jaw to the jaw angle, where Jiache S6 is located. It then ascends along the front of the ear to reach the hairline at the side of the forehead. From the side of the lower jaw, it descends along the neck and reaches the chest, moving along the nipple line. Turning inward, it runs over the abdomen to cross the groin to the front of the thigh, running along the side of the tibia, where Zu-Sanli S36 is found, 3 inches (8 cm) below the knee. The channel ends at the second toe, joining the spleen channel at Yinbai SP1.

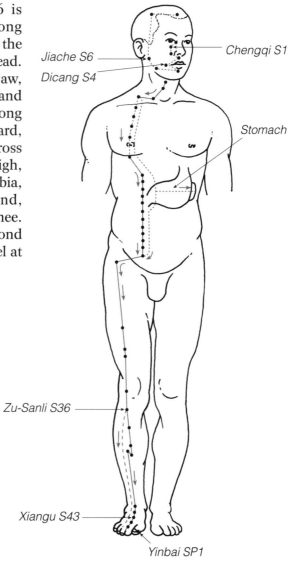

Jiache S6

Dicang S4

Chengqi S1

Stomach

Zu-Sanli S36

Xiangu S43

Yinbai SP1

THE SPLEEN CHANNEL OF FOOT TAIYIN

The spleen channel starts at the medial side of the big toe and runs along the side of the foot, where Taibai SP3 is found. It ascends along the medial side of the leg and the anterior of the thigh, passing across the groin to the abdomen. It continues upward, passing through the diaphragm and ascending along the oesophagus to reach the sides of the tongue. Another branch turns into the body cavity: one part of it connects to the spleen and communicates with the stomach, while another runs upward to connect with the heart channel.

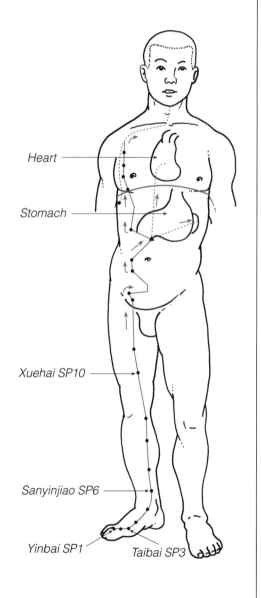

Heart

Stomach

Xuehai SP10

Sanyinjiao SP6

Yinbai SP1

Taibai SP3

THE HEART CHANNEL OF HAND SHAOYIN

The heart channel begins at the heart and runs inside the body to communicate with the small intestine. A second branch runs upward along the oesophagus to the eye. The main channel runs transversely from the heart to the lung, emerging from the armpit and passing along the medial side of the forearm to reach the wrist, where Shenmen H7 is found, ending at the lateral side of the tip of the little finger and connecting with the small intestine channel.

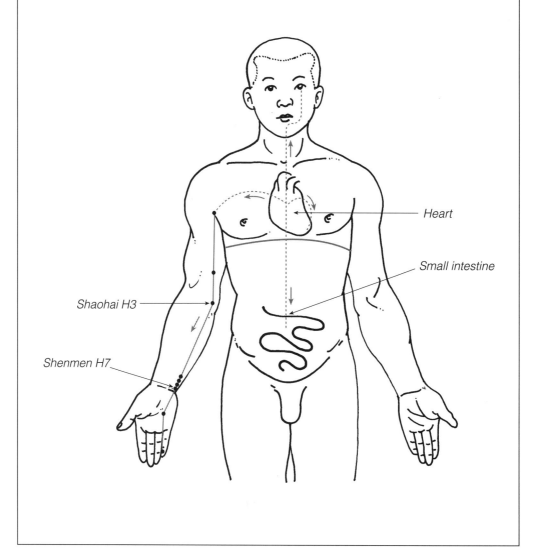

THE SMALL INTESTINE CHANNEL OF HAND TAIYANG

The small intestine channel starts at the medial side of the tip of the little finger at Shaoze SI1 and follows the medial side of the palm, where Houxi SI3 is found. It runs up the medial side of the forearm to the inner side of the humerus to the back of the shoulder. It then ascends along the neck to the cheek and ends at Tinggong SI19. From Quanliao SI18 it connects with the bladder channel at Jingming B1. A second channel branches at the supraclavicular fossa to enter the chest, joining the heart and running down to reach the small intestine.

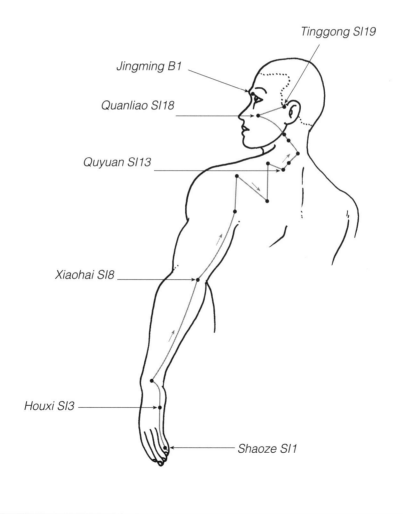

Tinggong SI19

Jingming B1

Quanliao SI18

Quyuan SI13

Xiaohai SI8

Houxi SI3

Shaoze SI1

THE BLADDER CHANNEL OF FOOT TAIYANG

The bladder channel starts at the inner side of the eye at Jingming B1 (see small intestine channel, page 53) and ascends to the forehead, where it joins a parallel channel at Baihui G20 (see Governor meridian). Here a branch splits off to the temple. The main channel enters the brain from Baihui G20 and re-emerges, bifurcating at the back of the neck and running down the side of the vertebral column to the lumbar region, where it reaches the bladder at Shenshu B23. The same channel then descends through the buttocks and terminates at the back of the knee. The branch from the neck runs parallel to the first channel on the lateral side and goes to the buttocks, turning laterally at the hip. It joins the main channel at the knee, at Weizhong B40, and follows the calf to the lateral side of the small toe, finally connecting with the kidney channel at the side of the fifth toe.

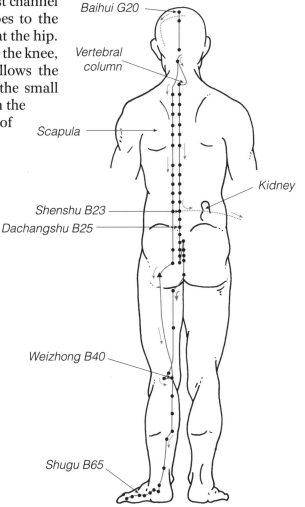

Baihui G20

Vertebral column

Scapula

Kidney

Shenshu B23

Dachangshu B25

Weizhong B40

Shugu B65

THE KIDNEY CHANNEL OF FOOT SHAOYIN

The kidney channel starts at the side of the small toe. It proceeds to the centre of the sole, where Yongquan K1 is found, and continues to the medial side of the foot at Taixi K3. From there it continues up the medial side of the knee and thigh and enters the body from Changqiang G1 at the perineum, ascending to the kidneys to communicate with the bladder. Re-emerging from the kidneys, it runs upward to enter the lung, continuing up to the throat and terminating at the root of the tongue. A branch diverts from the lung and joins the heart, connecting with the pericardium channel. The main channel ascends from the groin to the abdomen, ending at Shufu K27 below the clavicle.

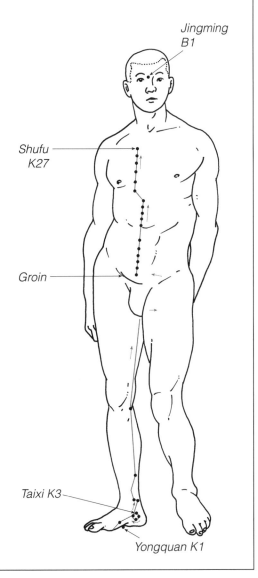

Jingming
B1

Shufu
K27

Groin

Taixi K3

Yongquan K1

THE PERICARDIUM CHANNEL OF HAND JUEYIN

The pericardium channel begins at the chest, where it connects with its organ, the heart. It descends into the abdomen, linking to the triple warmer (Sanjiao). The chest branch emerges at a point 3 inches (8 cm) below the anterior axillary folds and ascends, curving around the axilla, or armpit, to go down the middle of the arm and forearm between the lung and heart channels. It continues to the palm, ending at the tip of the middle finger. A second branch goes from Laogong P8 at the centre of the palm to the tip of the ring finger, where it connects with the triple warmer (Sanjiao) channel at Guanchong TW1.

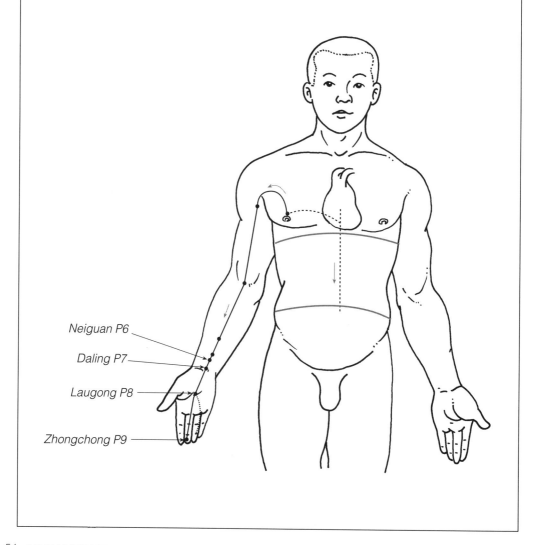

Neiguan P6

Daling P7

Laugong P8

Zhongchong P9

THE TRIPLE WARMER (SANJIAO) CHANNEL
OF HAND SHAOYANG

The triple warmer (Sanjiao) channel starts at the outer side of the tip of the ring finger at Guanchong TW1 and runs up to the dorsum of the hand and wrist, along the posterior side of the forearm and arm to reach Jianliao TW14 at the shoulder. From there it runs up the shoulder to the back of the neck, turning behind the earlobe to terminate at Sizhukong TW23 at the end of the eyebrow, where it connects with the gall bladder channel. A branch diverges at the supraclavicular fossa to go into the chest, joining up with the pericardium and then descending into the abdomen, where it connects to the peritoneal cavity and the triple warmer (Sanjiao).

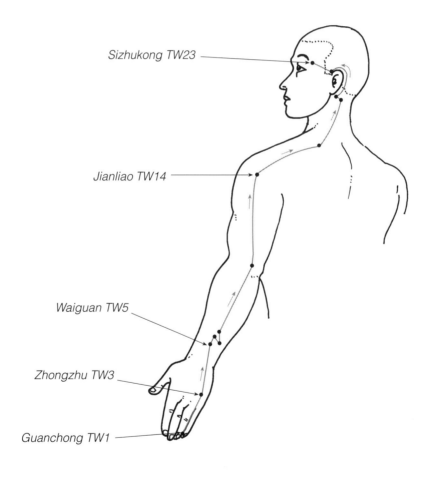

Sizhukong TW23

Jianliao TW14

Waiguan TW5

Zhongzhu TW3

Guanchong TW1

THE GALL BLADDER CHANNEL OF FOOT SHAOYANG

The gall bladder channel originates at the corner of the eye at Tongziliao GB1 and runs down the cheek to the front of the ear, making a few zigzag paths on the side of the head. From the occiput, or back of the head, it courses down the neck to the shoulder at Jianjing GB21 and goes down to cross over the clavicle to the side of the chest. From there it descends across the abdomen to the hip, where Huantiao GB30 is situated. From Huantiao GB30 it goes down the lateral side of the thigh to the knee and leg, and follows the lateral side of the foot to end at Zu-Qiaoyin GB44. A branch from the supraclavicular fossa passes into the chest and abdomen to connect with the liver. A branch at the dorsum of the foot bifurcates at Zu-Linqi GB41 to connect to the liver channel at Dadun Liv1 on the big toe.

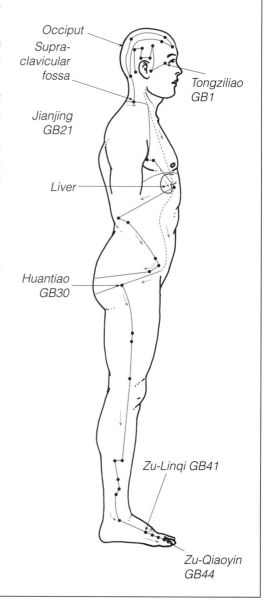

Occiput

Supra-clavicular fossa

Tongziliao GB1

Jianjing GB21

Liver

Huantiao GB30

Zu-Linqi GB41

Zu-Qiaoyin GB44

THE LIVER CHANNEL OF FOOT JUEYIN

The liver channel starts at Dadun Liv1 at the dorsal end of the big toe, passing upward to Zhongfeng Liv4. It ascends along the medial side of the knee and thigh to the pubic region, where it turns around to run upward to the side of the abdomen, reaching a point just below the breast. A branch from the lower abdomen turns inward to circle the stomach before reaching the liver and gall bladder. From the liver it passes upward to the throat, connecting with the eye and emerging at the forehead, finally connecting with the Governor meridian at the top of the head. Another branch goes from the liver to connect with the lung channel.

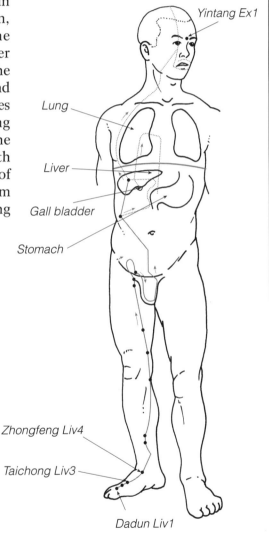

Yintang Ex1

Lung

Liver

Gall bladder

Stomach

Zhongfeng Liv4

Taichong Liv3

Dadun Liv1

The Extra Meridians

The eight extra meridians are special pathways for regulating qi in the 12 main channels. They also act as a reservoir for qi. They are Du Mai (Governor meridian), Ren Mai (Conception meridian), Dai Mai (Belt meridian), Chong Mai, Yinwei Mai, Yangwei Mai, Yinchiao Mai, and Yangchiao Mai. With the exception of the Governor and Conception meridians, they do not connect directly to the organs and do not have their own acupuncture points. They mingle among the 12 main channels and make use of the channels' acupuncture points to form their own pathways. For this reason, the extra meridians do not follow the qi circulation of the 12 main channels and the Governor and Conception meridians.

The Governor and Conception Meridians

Both the Governor and Conception meridians start inside the chest and branch out of the perineum externally. The Governor meridian flows upward along the spine to the top of the skull at the central line, ending at the centre of the upper lip. The Conception meridian comes out of the perineum, following the middle of the abdomen and chest to end at the lower lip.

The normal flow of qi is from the perineum upward for both meridians. Qigong exercise alters this flow by forcing the qi in the Governor meridian to jump over the upper lip and join the Conception meridian at the lower lip, thus forcing the qi to flow downward in the Conception meridian. Qigong increases qi until it is strong enough to jump across to the starting point of the Governor meridian, forming a circuit of flow called the small circle of Heaven. To reach this stage of Qigong practice is a big achievement and the aim of the exercise. The Governor meridian is the controller of all the yang channels in the body. The Conception meridian is the sea of all the yin channels. When the 12 channels are full of qi, the qi is directed to flow to the Governor and Conception meridians to be stored up. If the 12 channels are deficient in qi, qi from these two reservoirs flows out to supply them. The joining of these two meridians means the pooling of two reservoirs, which increases storage capacity. It also results in better control of the 12 main channels.

Dai Mai, the Belt Meridian

The Belt meridian starts from the side of the abdomen below the rib cage. It follows the iliac ridge of the groin, circling around the lower abdomen to the back. It is confluent with three gall bladder points, and regulates mainly the liver and gall bladder. It is the only pathway that runs across the body instead of longitudinally, cutting and encircling all the 12 channels in the body trunk and therefore communicating with all 12 channels. Qigong exercise makes use of this meridian to increase the flow of qi to the kidneys, adrenal glands, intestines, pancreas, liver, and genital organs. Kong Jing Qigong includes a "rolling the ball" step to link up the energy flow in the 12 main channels and strengthen the circulation to establish the great channel circle.

THE GOVERNOR MERIDIAN

The Governor meridian starts in the pelvic cavity, as does the Conception meridian, and emerges at the perineum to ascend along the spinal column, communicating with the kidneys. It continues to the brain, up to the top of the head, and then comes down along the front of the head and the nose to end at the upper lip.

There are 28 points along the Governor meridian. Points 1 to 4 control the urogenital system; points 5 to 7 are associated with the gastrointestinal organs; points 8 to 13 control the respiratory system; and points 14 onwards are involved with the brain.

The Chinese character for this meridian means "govern". The Governor meridian has the task of governing all the yang channels.

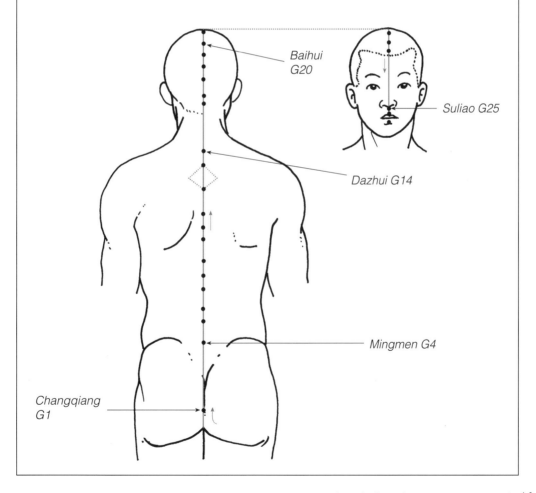

Baihui G20

Suliao G25

Dazhui G14

Mingmen G4

Changqiang G1

THE CONCEPTION MERIDIAN

The Conception meridian starts from the pelvic cavity, emerging at the perineum to run upward along the central line of the body over the abdomen and chest to the throat. It ends just below the lower lip.

There are 24 acupuncture points along this channel. Points 1 to 7 control diseases of the urogenital system; points 8 to 14 control the gastrointestinal system; and points 17 to 22 control the respiratory system. The most common points used in acupuncture are Tiantu C22, Shanzhong C17, Zhongwan C12, and Guanyuan C4.

The Chinese character for this meridian means "responsibility". The Conception meridian is responsible for all the yin channels.

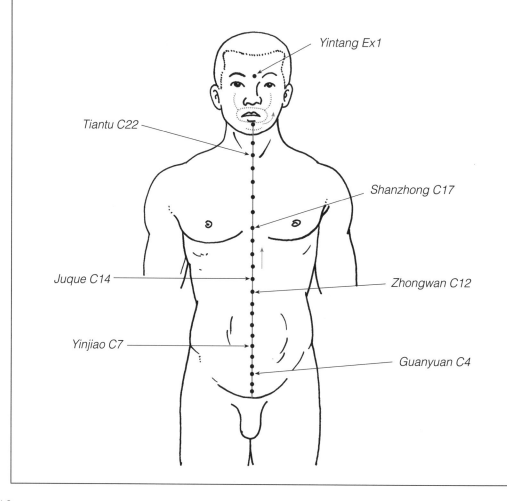

Where Are the Channels?

Although acupuncture and Qigong exercise have been practised in China for the past few thousand years, and also have been introduced to the western world for more than a hundred years, their rightful status in the medical field has not yet been established. The main obstacle lies in the lack of anatomical proof of the structure of the energy channels. In addition, qi cannot be identified visually. Many studies have been carried out in the past. The last one was done in Korea in the early 1960s. All efforts using scalpel and microscope proved futile. In the past two decades, however, separate studies using X-rays were successfully carried out in Taiwan and France (a college of acupuncture has been in existence for more than 120 years in France). An opaque substance was injected into the skin, aiming at the acupuncture point, while a control point was given the same substance. The acupuncture point collected the opaque substance at a small round area of about a centimetre and even ran up the channel about an inch, whereas at the control point the substance dispersed diffusely.

The Change of Tendon Classic, written by Da Mol two thousand years ago, defined quite specifically the connective tissue, the tendons, and the fascia as the tissues that serve as pathways for the circulation of qi. It is a wonder how this monk and Qigong master could define so specifically the existence of energy channels in connective tissue without the help of scientific instruments.

Now, let us review our modern medical knowledge of the structure of the connective tissue. Connective tissue forms a matrix of fibrous and cellular material in which more highly organised structures such as muscles, blood vessels, and nerves are embedded. In some places, it becomes condensed into a firmly woven texture of tough fibrous sheets termed fascia. Histologically, fascia contains fibres and cells embedded in a substratum of semi-gelatinous substance which is homogeneous in structure. This ground substance is a fine reticulum, the meshes of which contain tissue fluid. This fluid, which is partly derived from blood plasma containing protein, glucose, electrolytes, and water, is regarded as an essential medium occupying the intercellular space of all tissue through which nutrition from the bloodstream reaches the cells and the waste products of cell metabolism are conveyed into blood and lymphatic capillaries. It is the same tissue fluid in the fascia that serves as the conductor of qi in the form of electricity.

Around muscles, the connective tissue becomes condensed to form sheaths and intermuscular septa. Over the limbs, the connective tissue is well defined as a tough sheet of white fibrous tissue, or the deep fascia. The deep fascia forms a non-elastic, tightly fitting sleeve that keeps underlying structures in position and preserves the characteristic surface contour of the limbs.

From the sheathing layer of deep fascia processes extend down among subject structure to form fascial septa which, in the case of the limbs, create a series of compartments containing separate muscle groups, bundles of vessels, and nerves. The fascial planes usually represent the course of the energy channel. Acupuncture points are located along this passage. The connective tissues from the muscles of the limbs join the body and body cavity. In the body cavity, they form serous sacs, which include pericardial, pleural, and peritoneal cavities.

I give this detailed description of connective tissue because Da Mol defined the connective tissue as the passageway for the energy channels. Connective tissue is the only tissue that penetrates every part of the body, which qualifies it to be a pathway for energy that must circulate throughout the body. Its content of tissue fluid, which includes electrically charged ions, fulfils the requirement for the transmission of energy in the form of electricity and electromagnetic force. The diaphragm fits the description for storage of electricity, similar to that of the eel, with its muscular makeup and a big piece of connective tissue. The diaphragm must therefore be the storage area for qi.

Because energy channels are located in the fascia, which is a sheet of tissue, their width is much greater than that of blood vessels and nerves. If this was not so, it would be very difficult for the practitioner to locate acupuncture points. Acupuncture points are oval, with the longer measurement along the track of the channel. The shorter end of the point is roughly $^1/_5$–$^2/_5$ inches ($^1/_2$–1 cm). The passage is easily traced by following the groove made by the two adjacent muscles, where the sheathing fascia of the muscles join to become deep fascia and dip down to form a fascial tube to encircle the nerves and blood vessels. This structure makes the qi flow along with the blood circulation, thus establishing a close relation between blood and qi and giving rise to the saying, "Qi is the commander of the blood." (The word *channel* is the most appropriate term to describe the energy circulatory system, the jing luoh. Qi flows in the fascia. Some of its electrically charged ions move in a disorderly way in the fascial sheet, but most are drawn by the electrical charge of the blood stream to follow the course of the blood vessels, like a channel in the fascia that surrounds the blood vessels.)

In recent years several studies in and outside China have shown that qi is electricity in the body produced by the contraction of somatic muscles, the flow of ions in the blood stream, the breakdown of glucose, and the inhalation of ion particles from the air. According to the laws of electricity, the movement of electricity produces an electromagnetic field around it. On the other hand, the movement of an electromagnetic field also produces electricity. Electricity and electromagnetic force are the same thing expressed in two forms. The qi that flows in the fascia along the energy channels also produces an electromagnetic field around the channel. This electromagnetic force or radiation, through the transformation of its yin-yang polarity at the end of each channel, produces the driving force to circulate the energy through the 12 main channels. It can also be sent out of the body through the acupuncture points as external qi. This external qi is received by the other person through his or her acupuncture point and passes into his body along the energy channels. Modern science calls this channel the electromagnetic receptor or transmitter, depending on whether it is receiving or sending out qi.

Qi Flow in the Channels

Each of the 12 main channels possesses its own energy field and yin-yang polarity of differing strength. The 12 main channels join to form a closed circuit, thus working as a unit under one control. Conditions in one affect the others, especially adjacent channels. Treatment of one can therefore give a similar benefit to other channels.

Qi circulates constantly in the 12 main channels, leading the blood to make 54 rounds in the body in 24 hours. Each channel has a peak flow of two hours in every 24 hours. During the peak flow period, the concerned channel is at its most susceptible to any influence on its flow of qi. This is the best time to perform acupuncture or Qigong exercises. The peak period follows the sequence of the channel circuit, starting with the lung channel at the early hours of 3 to 5 a.m.:

lungs 3–5 a.m. —> large intestine 5–7 a.m. —> stomach 7–9 a.m. —> spleen 9–11 a.m. —> heart 11 a.m.–1 p.m. —> small intestine 1–3 p.m. —> bladder 3–5 p.m. —> kidney 5–7 p.m. —> pericardium 7–9 p.m. —> triple warmer (Sanjiao) 9–11 p.m. —> gall bladder 11 p.m.–1 a.m. —> liver 1–3 a.m.

An experiment was carried out in which three electrodes were put at the top, midpoint, and end of the Governor and Conception meridians. The qi in these meridians was measured in terms of the electrical charge in the muscles under the electrodes. The rate of qi flow was found to be different in accordance with age, health, and development of the Qigong practice of the person. Usually it takes about a minute to complete a round in the "small circle", as the joining of these two central extra meridians is called.

In my own test, I used a metal chain with a small ring. I held the chain between the thumb and index finger, leaving the ring at the bottom end. After a short while, my external qi started to travel down the chain, making the ring swing back and forth. The swing started with small waves, increasing to a maximum, and then decreasing again, repeating itself in a wavelike pattern. The interval between the two maximum swings took about three minutes. From the above test, we can see that qi travels in a wavelike pattern similar to the sound wave or radio wave, but at a very slow rate.

Acupuncture Points: A Diagnostic Pointer

The 12 main channels are embedded deep down between the muscles. Along its course a channel will rise to just below the skin at an acupuncture point usually located at the gap between two big muscles where the fascia is situated.

It was found in experiments that the electrical potential at the acupuncture points along a channel is of a step-like voltage. The differing potential of various acupuncture points forms a human electrical field. The electrical field is strong during mental concentration and when a person is excited. The electrical resistance

THE CIRCULATION OF QI THROUGH THE DAY

This diagram shows the changes in qi circulation through a 24-hour cycle, indicating the time of peak flow in the channels, the circuit of flow between the channels, and changes in polarity from yin to yang and back. Peak flow occurs when qi circulation is most forceful in an organ. At this time, disease in that organ reaches a peak. Thus, gallstones are most painful between 1 and 2 a.m. Bronchial asthma sufferers' worst hours are typically between 3 and 5 a.m. At these peak hours, the organ is also at its most susceptible to any influences; it is the best time to treat disease with acupuncture or Qigong.

Qi runs in a wavelike pattern from yin to yang and back as it flows from one channel to another. This transmutation is what drives the qi through the channels. The greater the transmutation, the more powerful the circulatory force. The greatest change occurs between the heart channel and the small intestine channel, where it changes from lesser yin to greater yang. This occurs at noon, which coincides with the full yang of the energy from the sun. Noon is the best time to do Qigong to assimilate cosmic energy into the system. The next major change occurs between the liver and gall bladder channels: the lesser yang of the gall bladder channel changes to the absolute yin of the liver channel at midnight, which is also a good time to build up qi, this time using the new yang energy of the rising sun.

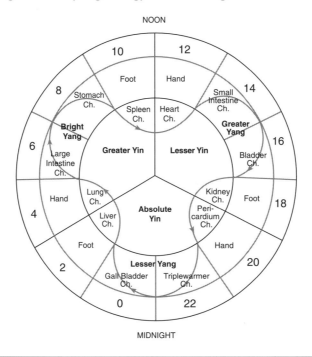

at a point is also lowered and the voltage increased when the organ associated with that point is sick. The point will become more tender than usual. Acupuncture points can thus serve as a mirror to reflect the condition of the organs in the body.

Channels and Energy Changes

Chinese medicine considers that qi is the essence of life and the controller of health. Sickness is due primarily to an imbalance or blockage of qi in the channel. If the qi is blocked, pain results. Pneumonia is not just due to an attack of bacteria or virus on the lung tissue. It is mainly due to an imbalance of qi in the lung channel, which weakens resistance and the immune system, giving hostile organisms a chance to break in and cause sickness. After all, pathological organisms and other aberrant qi like wind, dampness, and heat are around us all the time, usually without causing sickness.

Transmutation is the law of life and activity. When a force is applied to a big pool of water, it is broken up to produce yin and yang energy, which makes the water move up and down with the transformation of yin into yang and yang into yin. When an impulse is applied to one end of a muscle fibre, the negative charge inside the membrane of the fibre is changed to a positive one and the positive charge outside is changed to a negative charge. This changing of polarity produces an electrical current. Another example is seen in water. The radiation of the sun imparts yang energy to water on the earth, which originally possessed yin energy. As it receives more and more yang energy, it is changed into vapour, carrying the yang energy upward to the sky. On its way up, it loses its yang energy, leaving it with its own original yin energy. It then condenses to become water droplets and falls down to the earth again as rain.

The same law applies to qi in the human energy channels or meridians and explains why qi polarities change so much from one channel to another. It is this transmutation of qi polarities that produces the movement of qi and makes it circulate in the channel circuit. The only difference is that the polarity of human energy is more sophisticated in dividing into more grades of energy strength.

Yin and yang are further graded into greater, bright, and lesser yang, and greater, lesser, and absolute yin depending on their energy. They can be graded as follows:

greater yang	three yang	small intestine	bladder
bright yang	two yang	large intestine	stomach
lesser yang	one yang	triple warmer (Sanjiao)	gall bladder
greater yin	three yin	lung	spleen
lesser yin	two yin	kidney	heart
absolute yin	one yin	pericardium	liver

The greater the transmutation, the more powerful the energy change. The absolute transmutation of yin and yang energy is greatest at the heart and small intestine channels, where the lesser yin of the heart changes to the greater yang of the small intestine. The relative maximum change of the same energy occurs at the gall bladder and liver, from lesser yang to absolute yin. The peak flow of these two pairs of channels is from 11 a.m. to 1 p.m. for the heart and from 1 a.m. to 3 a.m. for the liver, which corresponds to the time of the greatest transmutation of nature's yin and yang energy at noon and midnight. These two periods are thus the best times either for acupuncture or Qigong exercise in the treatment of diseases.

Chapter 5

The Role of Qigong in Health

Qigong is the science of working with qi and the human energy field. In ancient China, Qigong was known as leading and running the qi. Through Qigong practice, qi is made to flow along the jing luoh, the energy channels, to exert its energy and regulating power and keep the body in good health.

Since the *Change of Tendon Classic* and the *Marrow Cleansing Classic*, written by Bodhidharma, better known as Da Mol, Qigong has been classified into Nei Kung, or internal exercise, and Wai Kung, or external exercise. The difference between them is in the degree of movement. External exercise is primarily a martial art, the hard-moving form for fighting techniques and the training of limbs to become very forceful, enabling the person to break bricks and stones. Internal exercise can be divided into meditation, which practises stillness and tranquillity, and Qigong, which falls between these two extremes and is practised mainly for health and longevity.

The Difference between Exercise and Qigong

Whenever health and exercise are raised as topics, the relative merits of physical exercise and Qigong are discussed. Physical exercise and games are easy to learn, interesting because of their competitive nature, and more lively, with larger amplitude of movement. They consume great amounts of energy, burn off cholesterol, and reduce hypertension and obesity. They activate muscle receptors to make use of insulin and improve diabetic control. One feels fresh and energetic with improved appetite after games or exercise, but they should be carried out in moderation or else they will do more harm than good.

Let us review the physiological changes during strenuous exercise and competitive games such as running, basketball, badminton, and football. The body systems are geared to give maximum capacity of the skeletal muscles for the best performance. The brain is tense and excited and exerts control and coordination for the same purpose. The sympathetic autonomic nervous system is activated for emergency action, which brings about the following:

- Increased cardiac contraction, giving more pumping force and an increased supply of blood to the skeletal muscles.
- The coronary artery and the blood vessels on the surface of the body are dilated to meet the demand for increased blood supply to the heart and body.
- The respiratory rate is increased to obtain more oxygen from the air to supply muscles during faster metabolism and eliminate waste products from the body.
- Other systems, including the stomach and intestines, are slowed down to spare blood for the skeletal muscles.

The joints of the lower limbs, which carry the whole weight of the body, receive all the pounding force in games and exercise.

A young and strong heart can bear the increased workload and recover from fatigue easily, and the blood vessels can absorb the increased force of the blood smoothly. But for an aging heart that has been working almost nonstop, the extra demand is hard to bear and the heart may fail to function. The degenerated blood vessels, which have thickened due to deposition of cholesterol, and lost their elasticity, may find it difficult to stand the increased force of the blood, causing a heart attack or stroke. These are seen frequently in sports.

Qigong exercise aims for health in the same way as physical exercise and games, but it is carried out in a different way:

- Qigong builds and conserves energy, unlike games, which use energy to produce movement.
- Unlike games, which require concentration, Qigong requires total relaxation of the mind, which should think of nothing. The skeletal muscles are relaxed as much as possible with just enough contraction of the muscles to keep the body in a fixed posture and cultivate qi.
- The parasympathetic autonomic nervous system is called to action to conserve energy. The contracting force of the heart is reduced, and the respiration slows down. The gastrointestinal system is brought into action.
- Qigong is an internal exercise. Movement of the body is kept to a minimum. If there is movement at all, it is used to lead and adjust the qi in the body. Physical exercise and games are more for training of the skeleton and its muscles. Qigong is the "exercise" of the organs directly under the control of the brain.
- The basis of Qigong exercise is the training of the mind. The Chinese believe that extreme emotions, such as anger, worry, sadness, joy, and fear, cause damage to the liver, spleen, lungs, kidneys, and heart, and are the internal cause of many diseases. Qigong makes one less easily agitated and is helpful in the control of cancer and other sicknesses. Training of the mind is important in external qi therapy to control the output of qi to the patient.

Qigong practice can achieve much more than physical exercise and games in the quest for health. Qigong can treat sickness and is used as an alternative to modern medicine, especially for chronic diseases. It has a rejuvenating effect and promotes longevity.

Physiological Changes During Qigong Exercise

During Qigong exercise, a person appears calm and relaxed with very little body movement, yet he sweats like someone who has just run a hundred-metre race. With the production of qi and its circulation in the channels, many physiological changes occur inside the body that continue even after the exercise stops.

• Qi

The production of new qi reinforces existing qi in the channels and one feels its existence with a sense of numbness, distension, heaviness, and itchiness along the track of the channel. If a person is not in good health, his or her extremities, especially the hands, will feel cold or pale even in warm weather. When he or she starts to do Qigong, cold air can be felt coming out of the hands. This cold air is called aberrant qi. The sicker the person, the more aberrant qi will come out. When health returns, the hands become warm again, and the qi also becomes warm. In a patient with arthritis of the knee, for instance, the knee will feel painful during Qigong exercise, with emission of cold air from the knee.

• Sweating

This is the first sign to appear in Qigong exercise. The sweat is profuse, even though there is no body movement, indicating that something is happening internally. Initially this sweat is foul-smelling. Sweating is strong on the head, back, and arms, while the palms are totally dry and warm. This is a strange phenomenon, as the sweat glands are distributed most densely in the palms. However, vapour comes from the tips of the fingers, looking like smoke from the lit end of a cigarette dancing up to the air.

• Heat

Heat is produced along with sweat. This heat is focused at the palms, where the temperature may be increased by 2–3° C. The raised temperature may continue even after the exercise stops. It is possible to feel the heat from a Qigong master at a distance of a few feet. Students of Qigong feel that their bodies have become quite warm and do not feel the cold so much.

• Breathing

Respiration becomes long, smooth, and gentle, with increased efficiency in the gaseous exchange of blood. Qigong emphasises slow, smooth, and gentle breathing with prolonged expiration. During expiration the parasympathetic nervous system is activated, lowering blood pressure, decreasing heart rate, and increasing gastric secretions. Movement of the diaphragm is extended. Movement of the bronchial lining increases, helping to expel discharge from the bronchial tree.

• Gastrointestinal system

Peristaltic movement increases and digestive function improves. Secretion of saliva, hormones, and enzymes increases. Flatulence frequently occurs, but it is odourless, indicating that it is due to increased intestinal movement, not bacterial fermentation.

• Heart and blood vessels

The contracting force of the heart muscle is reduced, although the force of the blood is increased due to the electromagnetic force produced by the qi along the blood vessels. Blood vessel capacity expands. The permeability of the blood vessel walls increases, which increases blood volume at the capillary end. This is seen especially in the hands, where the increase may be as much as 30 percent. The hands therefore look red and feel warm. This may explain why the palms do not sweat; they are too warm to allow condensation. Instead the sweat evaporates as vapour from the fingertips.

• Blood

Red blood cells and haemoglobin in the blood increases. Rosy cheeks appear on previously pale faces after two months of practice, without any addition of iron or protein in the diet. The level of antibodies, white blood cells, and interferon also rises, indicating enhanced immunity.

• Central nervous system

In the running of the qi, the emphasis is on tranquillity, emptiness, transparency, steadiness, and righteousness. Qigong aims at the brain as the target of exercise.

The human being has the most comprehensive living body. Under the same natural conditions man receives many more disturbing codes than other animals do. Humans are able to survive because they possess a highly developed central nervous system, a brain that can think, and a pair of hands to carry out the instructions from the brain. Functionally, the brain and its nervous system are concerned with the reception and integration of sensory information from all parts of the body and with producing responses appropriate to the sum of the sensory information reaching it at any moment, in the light of past experience.

Human life, especially a healthy life, depends on stable conditions in which to carry out the life processes. This stable state is termed homeostasis, or in traditional Chinese medicine, the balance of yin and yang energy in the body. The brain is the control centre of this homeostatic system. The jing luoh is its regulating system, and qi is the life code that maintains the system.

Acupuncture and Qigong in Qi Regulation

Acupuncture and Qigong exercise are used to correct imbalances or obstructions in the qi flow in order to return the body to normal health. Acupuncture makes use of metal needles to prick acupuncture points, stimulating energy in the channel by manually twitching the inserted needle or using an electrical stimulator. The qi is thus strengthened and adjusted.

Qigong exercise plays its greatest role in the treatment of chronic diseases. Its first concern is to build up the energy in the 12 main channels. When the qi is full in the main channels, which takes about two months of daily practice, it will then lead the external qi coming out of the palm to feed back to the body.

In a number of scientific studies, it was found that most messages coming to or from the brain come from or go to the hands (about one third), primarily the palms. The mind can therefore send an electromagnetic message to the palms directing the qi to move in a particular direction.

There are six main channels running from the arm to the hand, ending at the fingertips. Each channel carries with it energy of different grades of yin and yang. It is at the end of the fingers that the transformation of the energy polarity from dominantly yin to dominantly yang or from yang to yin takes place. The electromagnetic field in the hand is therefore stronger than in any other part of the body. It is for the same reason that Qigong masters always use their palms to send out external qi to treat patients. In Qigong practice, the palm is often placed over an acupuncture point or along an energy channel so that external qi coming from the palm can exert an enforcing energy to strengthen the flow of the qi and adjust any energy imbalance. One example is the creation of a closed circuit between the Governor and Conception meridians by placing the palms over the nose and leading the qi from the Governor meridian to jump to the lower lip, forcing the qi in the Conception meridian to reverse its original upward flow, forming a one-way circulation of the two major meridians.

The fingertip is the spot where the transmutation of energy polarities takes place. Close to this spot, there is a point just before the end of the channel where the change of energy is beginning to occur. This point is important as it can influence the transmutation significantly, and it is very often used in acupuncture and Qigong exercise. There are six such acupuncture points along the six main channels in the upper limbs, called Shu points. Three of the yin points are grouped on the palm side of the wrist: Shenmen point for the heart, Taiyuan for the lung, and Daling for the pericardium channels. The three yang points are Sanjian for the large intestine channel, situated at the proximal part of the index finger, Zhongzhu for the triple warmer, and Houxi for the small intestine, all placed at the proximal part of the fingers concerned.

This method of Qigong exercise is called conducting qi through the limbs. Depending on the condition of the qi, this method can be used to adjust the energy in the channel individually by flexing each finger separately or together in a small group. The ultimate aim of Qigong exercise is to create the small circle of Governor and Conception meridians and then a smooth and powerful energy flow in the big circle involving all the 12 main channels in order to keep the body healthy, to treat sickness, and to prolong life.

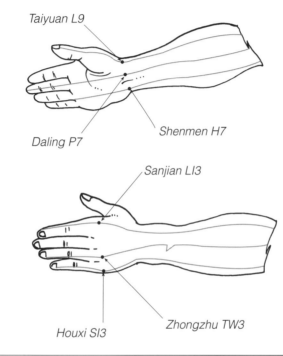
Effects of Qigong on Brain Waves

In recent years, research has been done on the effects of Qigong on brain activity, as reflected by electroencephalographic waves (EEG). The EEG of children shows primarily slow waves, while those of adults are faster. The general rule is that the rate becomes faster and the amplitude smaller with increased age. Qigong can reduce the rate and increase the amplitude of brain waves.

Qigong makes electrical activity of the brain cells become orderly. It also synchronises and stabilises brain cell activity in different sections of the brain, even in the presence of disturbance from light and noise. The more accomplished a person is in Qigong exercise, the more orderly is the brain activity. As a result, the electromagnetic force of the brain becomes stronger, and the electromagnetic field is many times bigger than that of an ordinary person.

Life depends on orderliness. From foetus to youth, this orderliness increases, until it reaches a state of perfection. From adolescence to old age, this orderly state steadily disintegrates. Body function degenerates, eventually bringing life to the edge of destruction. This is similar to the Chinese theory based on transmutation of yin and yang energy, explained in the previous chapter. Qigong, being able to make the electrical activity of brain cells orderly, improves the quality of life.

In recent years, western medicine has turned its attention to emotional and psychological factors as a cause of disease. Strong feelings of worry or excitement can interfere with digestion. Tension headaches, which have been associated with visceral factors, are all too common. Through medical research, it has been found that 50–80 percent of all diseases are due to mental tension. Typical examples are high blood pressure, migraine, chronic fatigue syndrome, and neurosis.

Mental disturbances and emotional upsets have long been recognised in China as causes of disease. Anger hurts the liver and makes qi from the liver gush up to the head, causing one to faint. Exhilaration hurts the heart by dispersing the qi from the heart. It may even make the heart stop contracting. Fear injures the kidneys and pushes qi down, resulting in loss of urinary control. These are exactly what modern medicine attributes to emergency action of the sympathetic nervous system with increased hormonal secretion of the adrenal glands, increased pulse and respiratory rates, peripheral blood vessel dilation, increased blood pressure, and elevated blood glucose.

Most of the organs in the body are served by the autonomic nervous system, also known as the vegetative or involuntary nervous system. It is called vegetative because it is concerned with growth and nutrition. It is involuntary because it functions independently of the central nervous system. It controls mainly the heart, blood vessels, glands, and smooth muscles and is categorised into the sympathetic and parasympathetic nervous systems. These function antagonistically, producing opposite effects on the organs that they both supply. Under natural conditions, the systems act synergistically—they cooperate to achieve the desired end. When a person falls ill or encounters a situation that requires emergency action, sympathetic control then comes to play, resulting in an increase in blood pressure and reduced peristalsis. Qigong exercise can reduce the activity of the sympathetic nervous system and raise the synergistic action of the two autonomic systems. Scientists have confirmed this using blood tests, which show that after Qigong exercise the level of the hormone prolactin in the blood is elevated, indicating the inhibition of dopamine activity, which is the stimulator of the sympathetic nervous system. The 5-hydroxytryptamine metabolism is increased, and the adrenal cortical hormone decreases by 50 percent. This is what makes a person relaxed and calm.

The influence of Qigong on the central nervous system can be illustrated in the close relationship between the rate and amplitude of brain waves and emotional changes. When a person is agitated or depressed, low-amplitude, fast-frequency brain waves appear. When his mood has calmed, slow waves reappear. A number of tests have been carried out outside China to measure the effects of Qigong on brain function. It was found that the EEG of a Qigong master is a slow-frequency, high-amplitude wave. The amplitude is three times that of an ordinary man, and is synchronised. Brain waves during Qigong exercise are different from those of a person in wakeful condition, resting, or in sleep. The alpha wave period is prolonged, the amplitude is increased, and the frequency is slower. The appearance of theta waves is in the presence of alpha waves. The EEG shows that during Qigong exercise, the suppressive alpha wave amplitude is increased and the rhythm is slower, indicating that the suppressive process is strengthened to protect overexcited brain cells from running chaotically, while allowing them to recover.

In May 1974, an interesting experiment was carried out in a university in Switzerland to find out the effect of Qigong on brain waves. It was discovered that Qigong can reduce the frequency and increase the amplitude of brain waves. The amplitude can be increased from that of an ordinary person's amplitude of 50 microvolts to 180 microvolts, a threefold increase. The brain, as the control centre for all the activities in the body, can be tuned by Qigong to bring it back to its childhood efficiency, thus reversing the direction of the degenerative process. This may explain how Qigong can increase longevity and make one young again.

The more important discovery from this experiment was that of the possibility of synchronizing waves of electricity from the various regions of the brain. This indicates that the electromagnetic field of brain cell activity has been regulated to become more orderly, thus increasing the electrical force of the brain.

Qi and Heart Disease

From scientific research in recent decades, qi has been found to consist of electricity and electromagnetic force. Electricity is produced during Qigong exercise by the contracting muscles, and flows in the fascia along the blood vessels. This flow of electricity produces an electromagnetic force and gives a pulling force to the electrically charged blood cells and plasma in blood vessels, thus enhancing the strength of blood circulation. The extra pulling force of qi on the blood is of great use to the cardiovascular system.

Ordinarily, blood circulation depends on the force of the heart's pumping and the elasticity of the blood vessels. In heart failure, the heart muscle becomes hypertrophic and weak, and the elastic tissues of the blood vessels degenerate. The heart therefore fails to provide enough driving force for normal circulation. The failing heart resorts to increasing its pumping rate in order to provide enough blood, which eventually weakens the heart even more because of the increased workload. The blood flow becomes sluggish and accumulates in the lungs, the abdomen, and the limbs. Diffusion of fluid from the blood occurs and the lungs are filled with fluid, which hinders oxygen exchange. The peritoneal cavity is filled with fluid, and the abdomen becomes distended. The lower legs and feet become swollen with fluid in the tissue space. Modern medicine can get rid of the fluid with diuretics and enhance the heart's output of blood with drugs to strengthen the heart muscle contractions, but this only puts a greater burden on the weakened heart, which eventually will come to its final stage of fatigue and stop functioning, usually in five years.

When the electromagnetic pulling force from qi strengthened by Qigong exercise comes to the aid of the heart and the blood vessels, the workload can be lessened for the weakened heart and degenerated blood vessels, giving them a chance to recover. Qi can be built up through Qigong exercise. The stronger the qi, the less work the heart has to do. Qigong exercise is therefore a good remedy for heart disease. In the few cases of cardiac disease in my Qigong class, Qigong contributed much to cardiac stability. The most impressive was the case of a patient with congestive heart failure with pulmonary oedema, ascites, and oedema of the legs. Drugs were given as an emergency measure to get rid of the extra fluid. Qigong exercise was added later, and in two years, the patient was able to live normally without medication.

Qi and Blood Flow

Qi can serve as a third driving force for the cardiovascular system. Qigong exercise builds up qi in the body and improves blood circulation through the increase in this driving power. The increase in blood supply is most prominent at the extremities. It was measured in a scientific study that the supply of blood in the hand can increase by as much as 30 percent of its normal flow. The temperature in the palm is also increased by 2–3° C due to this increased blood supply. A warm hand signifies strong qi and good health.

Improved blood supply is of great importance in the joints because of constricted blood vessels. In the joints the bone and the synovial membrane are supplied with blood directly from the blood vessels. The cartilage, especially the inner part, is nourished by diffusion through the matrix. Whenever there is an insufficient supply of blood, the cartilage in the structure of the joint is the first to be affected. This often happens in elderly patients, whose blood vessels have become very narrow, with reduced blood supply, due to degeneration. This is one of the causes of joint pain in the elderly. It is similar to calf muscle cramps in diabetics, whose blood supply to the muscles is reduced, while lactic acid, the waste product of metabolism, is not removed efficiently by the blood, causing contraction and pain in the calf muscle. A few students in my Qigong class recovered from their arthritis or diabetes-induced leg cramps after practising Qigong for only a few months.

Chapter 6

Kong Jing Qigong:
Preparation and Method

Qigong is an exercise to cultivate and regulate qi, or human energy. It is used to keep one in general good health, treat diseases, and attain a longer life. The method of Qigong differs according to the desired goal. Due to differences in concept, the method adopted to attain the same goal may vary.

There are many different schools of Qigong practice, but the fundamental principles are similar. Qigong practice is always based on control of the mind, breathing exercise, and regulating the body. Different schools may place different emphasis on these three components, but they all stress the same objectives of health, treatment of disease, and longevity.

Fundamental Principles of Kong Jing Qigong

The school of Qigong I advocate in this book is Kong Jing Qigong. This book is arranged and edited by Master Huang Jen Jong from Shanghai, China. He bases his work on the *Treatment of the Magic Palm* and the *Practice of the Internal Force*, both written by Da Mol (Bodhidharma) from the renowned Shaolin Monastery.

Kong Jing Qigong is an excellent exercise for old and young, healthy and weak. It requires little bodily exertion, is simple to learn, and has no adverse effects if followed correctly. The elementary course described here is intended especially for self-treatment of disease. Intermediate and advanced courses are reserved for treating diseases using external qi. The elementary course focuses on building and regulating qi. It is the most efficient technique for cultivating qi. If we grasp the three main principles of Qigong—regulation of mind, breathing, and body—we are on our way to success in the practice of Qigong.

Control of the Mind

The first principle is tranquillity, which means to keep the mind in a state of perfect calm, without any disturbing thoughts. In this condition, unhealthy emotions are reduced, and aberrant influences from the external environment and unwanted mental activity are minimized. This leaves the central nervous system free to regulate the functions of the various organs under its control and to maintain the balance of the endocrine system.

If sports and games can be classified as external exercise of the body, Qigong is then the internal exercise of the organs. Both produce heat and profuse sweating, although one involves a lot of movement while the other requires little bodily movement. The basic principle of Qigong is the training of the mind.

In recent years, much attention has been focused on psychosomatic disease, which reveals that the mind is an important factor in physiological and pathological changes in the body. An interesting study was carried out to prove this point by putting a goat and a wolf in adjoining cages and a second goat in a cage out of sight of the wolf. The isolated goat ate well and stayed healthy. The goat next to the wolf was agitated. It did not eat or sleep much and eventually died.

Extreme emotions cause physiological changes by shifting control of the organs in the body to the sympathetic nervous system, with increased secretion of adrenaline and cortisone. These are contributing factors in high blood pressure, peptic ulcers, and heart disease. Unstable emotions also lower the normal physiological functioning of the organs and immune system, and make endocrine secretion irregular. A recent study in the United States concluded that relaxation of the mind and body could enhance immunity.

Mental calm and resistance to internal emotional disturbances and thought, as well as external irritations and noise, are the keys to effective practice of Qigong. The mind is focused on learning Qigong, thinking only of the way to practise Qigong. It is only occasionally used to adjust and relax the body. The aim is to bring the conscious mind to a state between sleep and wakefulness, totally oblivious to what is happening around. This is the goal to attain for efficient Qigong practice. The qi built at this stage is potent. The sense of flowing qi in the body then becomes acute.

The feeling of mental calm varies with different people. Some feel so relaxed and comfortable that they want to continue the exercise. Others may feel as if the body is slowly growing taller, like a tree shooting up to the sky. The arms feel as if they could embrace a big building. Some may feel cold air coming out of the neck and back. The facial muscles may twitch, like a clown making faces. Most people, however, will feel that their mind has become very clear and transparent, and the body warm, light, and relaxed, with occasional muscle twitches. Sensations likened to an electric current pulsing through the body, a warm stream circulating, numbness, and itchiness are often experienced.

After mastering Qigong, you can learn how to use the mind to lead qi in the body and to experience the feeling of qi flowing to various parts of the body under the control of the mind. However, you should *never* use the mind to interfere with the natural circulation of qi, as this would lead to great trouble.

Some beginners may find it difficult to calm themselves for the practice of Qigong. This may be due to sickness, irritating light, noise, or weather (stuffiness, wind, heat, or cold). It may also be due to internal causes, such as worry, restlessness, or anger. Under such conditions it may be helpful to induce relaxation of the mind by a soft physical exercise, such as the Swinging Arms Exercise, described later in the chapter.

Regulating Breathing

Breathing exercise is important in Qigong as it is necessary to take in oxygen and charged ions from the air in order to produce qi.

Qi circulation relies on the force of respiration. If breathing is to be useful for Qigong practice, it has to be long, smooth, deep, and natural. Inhalation should be comparatively short and exhalation long. During exhalation, the central nervous system is stimulated and begins to shift the autonomic nervous system to the control of the parasympathetic nervous system, which lowers blood pressure, increases gastric secretions, and reduces the heart rate. These are often disturbed by unstable emotions.

Qigong influences bioelectricity in the body by lowering electrical resistance during exhalation and nearly doubling resistance during inhalation. Exhalation therefore favours bioelectrical flow.

During exhalation, the chest wall sinks down and in, and the diaphragm is raised. Compression of the chest cavity forces qi in the chest to flow down along the Conception meridian to the elixir field, the mesentery in the abdomen, to be stored up. Some also flows through the three yin channels in the arms to the fingertips. This makes the fingers feel warm and distended, with plenty of energy.

Some schools of Qigong emphasize breathing exercise and make use of the mouth and lips to produce resonance in the mouth cavity and give a different vibration to the palate, thereby stimulating the base of the brain to regulate qi. This is in fact just another method of forced exhalation.

The main purpose of the breathing exercise is to send qi to the elixir field to be stored. Exhalation leads the qi to flow along the Conception meridian to reach the elixir field by a short cut. We only need to pay attention to exhalation to achieve this aim.

In natural quiet breathing, inhalation is short and exhalation long. During Qigong exercise the respiratory rate becomes slower and exhalation is proportionally prolonged. Kong Jing Qigong therefore stresses natural breathing during exercise. Controlled breathing interferes with relaxation of the brain, and if not done properly, will give more trouble than good.

Adjusting the Body

This is the most important procedure in Qigong training. Since qi is mainly produced by contraction of the skeletal muscles, proper adjustment of the skeletal muscles is very important to the production of qi.

Kong Jing Qigong places great emphasis on the use of body adjustment to regulate the mind and breathing. Adjusting the body and its muscles properly results in the relaxation of the body. This has a calming effect on the central nervous system, which helps to control the mind. With relaxation of the brain, the parasympathetic autonomic nervous system takes over and produces a soft, slow, deep, long exhalation, thus regulating the breathing. Kong Jing Qigong has the advantage of regulating the breathing naturally without using the mind, thus enabling the central nervous system to attain the supreme stage of calm. The brain will be in a better state to serve as controller and coordinator of the various organs in the body.

A modern scientific study confirms that greater muscle relaxation promotes blood circulation in the body. If maximum tension of the muscles is rated as 100 percent, then 20–30 percent tension will begin to hinder blood circulation. When tension reaches 60–80 percent, blood circulation will stop altogether. When the muscles are relaxed, blood circulation increases by 15 to 16 times.

Muscle tension is directly under the control of the central nervous system. Therefore, excitement of the brain will lower blood circulation. It was also found that when the mind is calm, brain impulses direct the electrical flow in the muscles from centre to periphery, travelling in line with the blood flow and enhancing its circulatory force. According to Chinese medicine, when blood and qi are flowing together in a smooth and uninterrupted way, sickness will not occur.

Qigong depends on contraction of the muscles to produce bioenergy in the form of electricity. All the muscles in the body must be involved to get the maximum effect. Since the skeletal muscles are under the control of the central nervous system and represent the bulk of the muscles in the body, they must be motivated to produce bioenergy, or qi, by assuming a posture that involves the contraction of all skeletal muscles.

Posture

Posturing starts with relaxation of the whole body. Stand with feet parallel to each other at a distance equal to the width of the shoulders. Keep the body trunk straight and erect, with the shoulders dropped, to release tension in the arms and keep all the muscles of your body in equilibrium.

Raise both forearms with elbows bent at a 90° angle. Open the armpits by abducting the arm laterally, making the muscles on the forearms and upper arms contract. Push the forearms slightly forward. The shoulder muscles are thus activated. Keep palms facing down and wrists level, without bending up or down. Slightly abduct the fingers. This makes the muscles around the wrist and fingers contract equally and in equilibrium.

Bend both knees at a 30° angle. This brings the hip, knee, and ankle joints into action, involving all the muscles in the lower limbs. Rotate the hip joint outward, thus forcing the knee joints to turn out. This brings the muscles on the inner side of the thighs, the vastus and the magnus, into action.

Keep your body upright to force the back muscles to contract in support of the spine. Hold the chest slightly in to force the shoulder and upper back muscles to contract. The abdominal muscles can be mobilised by shifting the body weight onto the buttocks in the knee-bending posture, while rotating the hip joint outward. The head is held upright as if a string were pulling it up from the top of the skull. The eyes look straight ahead. This brings the muscles around the neck into action. With this standing posture, all the skeletal muscles are effectively brought into the process of producing electricity.

Relaxation

After all the skeletal muscles are mobilised through posturing, the second criteria is then brought into play. Contraction of the muscles is a prerequisite for the production of qi, but muscle tension must not be so great as to hinder the circulation of qi and blood. This can be accomplished by relaxing the muscles and releasing them from the control of the mind that initially brought them into contraction. The contraction of the skeletal muscles is then maintained by postural reflex, cutting off impulses from the brain to reach what Qigong masters call the state of force within relaxation.

This standing posture is very effective in producing qi and is used by many schools of Qigong as a fundamental stage in their Qigong practice. It is particularly important in Kong Jing Qigong because many procedures of the exercise are carried out in this posture to ensure qi is constantly produced for fingering movements.

Feedback

The most significant technique in Kong Jing Qigong is the regulation of qi through feedback in the channels. This is accomplished either through flexion of the fingers or by directing the qi in the palms to feed back to the channels at the acupuncture points. Feedback is a scientific term used to indicate that the output of a system is being sent back to the system to produce an enhancing or reducing regulating function. In the living body, biofeedback means that qi emitted from the palm or finger is sent back to the body through the acupuncture points and channels to bring qi circulation to a new balance and harmony. To carry out the feedback, the palm is placed over an acupuncture point or directly over the organ and left there for one to five minutes. The palm can also be moved along a particular channel to send qi in and regulate the existing flow of qi.

Fingering is a feature of Kong Jing Qigong that is different from other schools of Qigong. The fingers are bent at the joints, thus pulling the tendons to press on the acupuncture points around the wrist. The pressure on these points helps to adjust qi flow in the channels.

There are six special points in the upper limbs, one for each channel. They are important because they are the stations of the qi channels where the polarity starts to change from yin to yang or from yang to yin, and are therefore more sensitive to change. The points for the three yin channels are Taiyuan L9 for the lung channel, Daling P7 for the pericardium channel, and Shenmen H7 for the heart channel, all on the ventral side of the wrist. The three points for the yang channels are Sanjian LI3 for the large intestine channel, Zhongzhu TW3 for the triple warmer (Sanjiao) channel, and Houxi SI3 for the small intestine channel.

The standing posture may be difficult for the sick and aged. Posturing can also be done in a sitting position or even in bed, although the results will not be as good since not all the skeletal muscles are used.

Preparation

Kong Jing Qigong is a simple exercise and easy to learn. It requires little physical exertion and is composed of few movements. It does not require concentration and can thus be practised while watching television or talking to others. Some self-discipline is needed to carry on the exercise alone regularly for half an hour to one hour, and thus many find it easier to exercise in a group.

Things to Avoid

- Practising when one is sick or exhausted.
- Practising with a full stomach or within one hour after taking food.
- Drinking wine or beer just before or immediately after the exercise.
- Sex two hours before or after.
- Practising in a windy place. One falls sick easily, as skin pores are open wide.
- Drinking cold water or taking a cold bath within one hour.
- Practising barefoot or standing on cold ground. Shoes and full-length sportswear should be worn.
- Practising in an emotionally disturbed state.
- Practising when hungry. It is a good idea to drink warm milk or a nutritious drink just before the exercise.
- Practising in dirty surroundings or in a stuffy room.
- Exercising during a thunderstorm.
- Practising other forms of Qigong at the same time, especially those that stress mental concentration. It can be very harmful.
- Doing it halfway and stopping. If you must stop in the middle, the exercise should be completed later, especially if right and left movement is involved.
- Altering the sequence of movement. Follow the routine correctly and faithfully.
- Practising near high-tension electrical wires.
- Passing urine immediately after the exercise. This drains away some of the qi. It is better to empty the bowels before starting practice.

If the above advice is not followed, the result may be dizziness, nausea, or vomiting. Some people may feel chills, while others may experience headache.

Relative Positions and Best Times

- When several people are doing the exercise together, it is better to form a circle with everyone facing the centre. The qi that comes out of each person will pass around to form a qi field and strengthen everyone in the circle.
- If a person is doing the exercise alone it is better to stand facing either the north or the south. The body will be in line with the earth's magnetic field and can tap magnetic radiation to strengthen the body's electromagnetic field.
- A man should stand on the left side of a woman when they are practising Qigong together. In this way, their polarity will harmonise to benefit each other. Likewise, a wife should sleep on the right side of the husband to avoid sleep disturbances due to the imbalance of qi polarity between them.
- The best time to do Qigong exercise is at midnight, when the yin energy is diminishing and the fresh energetic new yang, influenced by the rising sun, is rising. The next best time is at noon, when yang qi has reached its maximum and is good for the heart, but it is inconvenient for most people as it occurs at mealtime. The alternative is 5–7 a.m. or 5–7 p.m.

Kong Jing Qigong

The primary course of Kong Jing Qigong is arranged specially for building up health and for the self-treatment of disease. It is composed of the following procedures:

1. Horse Stance Posture, for building qi
2. Arms Embracing the Moon, for biofeedback
3. Fostering Primordial Qi, for rejuvenation
4. Holding the Ball With Both Hands
5. Holding the Ball With Fingering
6. Rolling the Ball
7. Rolling the Ball With Fingering
8. Regulating Qi Through Three Entry Points.

The goals of Kong Jing Qigong are to bring in environmental external qi, which includes oxygen from the air, cosmic radiation, and the earth's magnetic radiation, and to send out qi from the body, which is used in the treatment of diseases.

WARNING: Do not use the mind to lead or influence qi circulation. Let the qi and blood flow in their own rhythm naturally during Qigong exercise and also when giving out qi to treat a patient.

Kong Jing Qigong follows the basic aims of Qigong exercise in regulating the mind, the breathing, and the skeletal muscles, but simplifies the procedure into one. It uses posturing to regulate the skeletal muscles, thereby calming the mind and regulating the breathing. In this way it cultivates and regulates the circulation of qi.

I. Horse Stance Posture

Swinging Arms Exercise

1. Keep the body upright and stand with feet parallel and apart at shoulder width. This brings the soles of the feet into maximum contact with the ground. Adjust the body weight equally on the feet, so that the centre of gravity falls in between. The body is thus very stable, with all the muscles in equilibrium (Fig. 1.1). Breathe naturally and try to relax the whole body. Drop the shoulders and bend the elbows slightly, turning them slightly outward. This will relax the shoulders, arms, and forearms. The body is ready to do the relaxing swinging exercise.

2. Lift both arms to shoulder level (Fig. 1.2).

3. Drop the arms smoothly to the thighs.

4. Turn the body to the left, bending the right knee. Let your body weight fall on your right foot. Use your turning motion to swing the right forearm up until the hand reaches the front of the left shoulder. The left forearm swings up the back to the lumbar spine. Keep your head facing front. (Figs. 1.3 and 1.4.)

5. Drop both hands and swing them back to the sides while turning the body to the front. The body weight shifts back to both feet. Drop the arms as in Fig. 1.1.

6. Lift both arms to shoulder level (Fig. 1.2).

7. Turn the body to the right, bending the left knee. Put your body weight on the left foot. Swing the left forearm up, left hand reaching the front of the right shoulder (Fig. 1.5). The right forearm swings to the back, touching the lumbar spine.

8. Drop both hands. Swing them back to the sides as the body turns back to the front. This completes the left and right swing.

9. Repeat the above procedure from (1) to (8). The swinging must be smooth, continuous, and slow with body, arms, and legs all relaxed. It takes about one second to make one right and left swing. Continue for 2–5 minutes.

Always perform the Swinging Arms Exercise before starting Qigong exercise.

1.1
Stand with feet apart at shoulder width. Relax the body.

1.4
Rear view of 1.3.

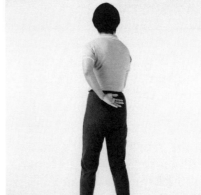

1.2
Lift arms to shoulder level.

1.5
Swing body to the right.

1.3
Turn body to the left, swinging arms up. Keep head facing front.

Horse Stance Posture

1. Continue from Swinging Arms Exercise. Stand with two feet parallel at shoulder width. Let the arms drop to the sides of the body and extend slightly from the armpits, with palms facing the thighs (Fig. 1.6).
2. Lift forearms with palms facing each other. The forearms should be parallel to each other and horizontal to the ground. Elbows are kept at a 90° angle. Bend the knees at a 30° angle, with the kneecaps lined up over the toes. The whole action takes about four seconds (Figs. 1.11 and 1.12).
3. Turn the palms slowly toward the ground (Fig. 1.13).
4. Extend the forearms sideways from the elbows about 30° (Fig. 1.14).
5. Bring the hands down and back toward the sides of the body while lifting up the elbows as in Fig. 1.15. Palms should face the back.
6. Flex the wrists up. Rotate the elbows to bring the fingers to point toward the waist. Stay for 10 seconds (Fig. 1.16).
7. Turn the elbows back and bring the arms and forearms to the sides, with the fingertips serving as a fulcrum (Figs. 1.17 and 1.18).
8. Release tension at the shoulders to allow the arms to push forward until the elbow is slightly in front of the body. The forearms should be parallel and horizontal (Fig. 1.19).
9. Turn both palms to face the ground, thus forming the Horse Stance Posture. Keep the wrists level, with the third finger in line with the forearm (Fig. 1.20) Do not lean back, as it will put the abdominal muscles out of contraction and result in a loose and distended abdomen (Fig. 1.21). Also avoid leaning forward. It slackens the chest muscles and reduces breathing (Fig. 1.22). The kneecap must not fall beyond the tips of the toes, as this would shift the centre of gravity in front of the feet and make the posture unstable (Fig. 1.23). It would also slacken the abdominal muscles.
10. Push the elbows slightly to the front. This puts the shoulder muscles into action. Bring the elbows slightly out sideways to make the inner arm muscles contract. Rotate the hip joints outward, turning the knee joints laterally. This will open up the buttocks and anus and bring the big muscles of the inner thighs into action. After assuming the proper posture, try to relax the whole body. Look ahead and focus on a distant object until the sight becomes cloudy. Half-close the eyes and relax the face muscles with a smile. This will in turn relax the whole body.

Practise the Horse Stance Posture for 30 minutes every day. This procedure should be carried on for a total of 15 hours for a healthy person before proceeding to the next step.

1.6
Beginning
posture.
Feet are
apart at
shoulder
width.

1.9
Lady hand
style (side
view).

1.10
Lady hand
style
(front
view).

1.7
WRONG
POSTURE.
Feet are
too wide
apart.

1.11
Lift
forearms.

1.8
WRONG
POSTURE.
Feet are
too close
together.

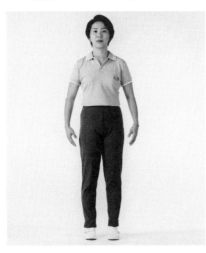

1.12
Side view
of 1.11.
Knees are
slightly
bent.

*1.13
Turn
palms
down.*

*1.16
Turn
hands up
with
fingers
pointing
at waist.*

*1.14
Extend
arms
sideways.*

*1.17
Bring
elbows in
to sides.*

*1.15
Bring
forearms
down.*

*1.18
Side view
of 1.17.*

1.19 Bring forearms to front.

1.20 Turn palms down.

1.21 WRONG POSTURE. Leaning backward.

1.22 WRONG POSTURE. Leaning forward.

1.23 WRONG POSTURE. Knees too bent, knees lined up beyond the toes.

Now we are in the Horse Stance Posture. All the skeletal muscles are involved in producing electricity, which is one of the elements of qi. It is very similar to the charging of a car battery. When the engine has started, just let it run to charge the battery. The longer the engine is running, the higher will be the charge. The body cannot be damaged by overcharging, as the channels and meridians can adjust energy production. Therefore, the longer one practises the Horse Stance posture, the stronger the energy. A stronger energy store is necessary to do the subsequent steps of feedback and adjustment of qi with fingering.

The beginner may find it hard to do the Horse Stance Posture for more than 15 minutes, but with practice this time will increase. Until one has practised the Horse Stance Posture for at least 30 minutes every day for a month (for a healthy person), or for two months (for the sick), it is not advisable to proceed to the second step, the energy feedback exercise.

The human storage of qi is huge. The main storage is situated in the diaphragm and the mesentery in the abdomen. The fascia, with its content of charged ions, is the subsidiary storage. The storage can rarely be overcharged as we are using the energy every second to power the organs in the body and losing energy in movement, exercise, and sexual activity.

Winding Up Procedure

Every time the Horse Stance exercise is completed, the qi that is running in the channels should be led to the elixir field to be stored up instead of being allowed to scatter. Be sure to end every Qigong session with this Winding Up Procedure:
1. From the Horse Stance Posture, close up the fingers to form a fist, as if holding an imaginary ball. This is to stop the qi from escaping from the fingertips and palms (Fig. 1.24).
2. Lift forearms to bring hands to the collarbone. Straighten from the knee-bending position. Take a long, slow, soft breath through the nose. The qi from the upper arms will come to the chest (Fig. 1.25).
3. Bring the hands from the collarbone down to the side of the thighs and open up the hands. Breathe out slowly from the mouth. This will bring the qi down to the abdomen to be stored in the elixir field (Figs. 1.26 and 1.27).
4. Relax and stand normally.

*1.24
Remaining
in the
Horse
Stance
Posture,
close
fingers.*

*1.26
Lower
forearms.*

*1.25
Make fists
and lift
forearms.*

*1.27
Lower
forearms
and return
to normal
stance.*

Theory and Mechanism of Action

Posturing is all that is needed to cultivate qi. It is a fundamental procedure for a number of Qigong schools. It is particularly important for Kong Jing Qigong, as posturing alone is able to fulfil the three principles of regulating the mind, breathing, and body in the process of building qi. Furthermore, the subsequent stages of Kong Jing Qigong are carried out in the Horse Stance Posture. Therefore, the Horse Stance Posture must be correct. As we have stressed previously, the correct posture should be based on:

- Mobilising all the skeletal muscles of the body,
- Relaxing the muscles and the mind to allow the smooth flow of qi,
- Biofeedback of the cultivated qi to regulate qi circulation, and
- Fingering to regulate individual channels in their change of polarity and qi flow.

Now let us review how posturing can affect the circulation of qi in the energy channels and meridians. The jing luoh has been classified into quite a comprehensive network, but for Qigong exercise we are only concerned with the 12 main channels and the two main meridians.

The two main extra meridians, the Governor and the Conception meridians, are the most important. Each of them starts from the perineum, the region in between the genital organs and the anus, and runs along the central line of the body, one in front and the other behind, to meet at the lips. The Governor meridian starts behind and ends at the upper lip. The Conception meridian runs in front to terminate at the lower lip. Qigong exercise aims to join the two meridians, making the qi circulate in one direction to form a closed circuit. This will make the qi circulation much stronger. As the Governor meridian communicates with all the yang channels and the Conception meridian controls all the yin channels in the body, improvement of the circulation in these two meridians will influence all the 12 main channels, thus enhancing qi flow in the whole body.

Relaxing the Lower Back

Because the lower limbs carry the weight of the body, it is rather difficult to relax their muscles. Yet relaxing these muscles is crucial for the smooth circulation of qi. If the thighs are not relaxed, the waist will be stiff and qi will find it hard to descend to the lower abdomen, where the elixir field is situated. This will result in sluggish circulation.

The waist can be made to relax by correct positioning of the nearby moveable bones, which have their muscles attached to the sacrum and pelvic bones.

1. Place the feet parallel to each other at shoulder width. This will relax the muscles of the hip.
2. Bend both knees slightly, about 30°, keeping the kneecap inside the tips of the toes. This will release tension in the thigh and calf muscles.

3. Make a dome at the buttocks by rotating the hip joints outward to open up the space between the thighs. This forms a round dome at the perineum. The anus will have a sensation of being opened. After this, turn the knees slightly inward until the soles are in contact with the maximum area of the ground.

In this posture, body weight is transferred from the centre, or the lumbosacral region, to the sides of the body, going down the thighs and legs. This relieves pressure on the waist and allows the waist to relax. Students in my class who did not follow this procedure correctly ended up with pain in the lower back or lower abdomen.

To Assess the Posturing Effect
In order to assess whether the posture is correct, watch for the following signs:
- If the posture is correct, the lower abdomen will automatically flatten.
- The hip and the knee joints have the feeling of sinking down slightly.
- The anus will feel more open, with an inner pulling force lifting it up.

It requires patience and constant practice to accomplish correct posture. It must be emphasized that all these effects of lifting up the anus, relaxing the waist, and sucking in the abdominal muscles must be achieved naturally, through proper positioning. If mental force is used, it will lead to stiffness and pain of the lower back and abdomen, resulting in constipation.

The movement used to bring the body to the Horse Stance Posture is called the starting procedure. This is done to start the production and circulation of qi in the body. The lifting of the forearms forces the qi in the lung channel to flow to the large intestine channel and follow the course of the big circulation to the last station of the liver channel, joining the lung channel to recycle through the 12 main channels. From the lower limbs, the natural arch of the sole makes the lateral edge of the foot bear most of the body weight. When the knees are bent, it stimulates the qi in the gall bladder channel situated at the side of the foot. Thus from the greater yin channel of the lungs to the lesser yang channel of the gall bladder, qi is being reinforced to strengthen energy circulation. When the fingers point to the waist in the starting procedure, they send out qi from the fingertips to stimulate the Belt meridian around the waist. It is through stimulation of the Belt meridian that the two main meridians and the six channels of the foot are motivated.

Important Points in Qigong Exercise
In Qigong exercise, the movement must be soft, slow, continuous, relaxed, and round. *Soft* means that the action should be gentle. *Continuous* and *slow* movements are required, to be in tune with the slow flow of the qi so that it can flow from the hand and the head to the foot. *Round* and *relaxed* movements are essential to reduce tight angles at the joints and tension in the muscles, which obstruct the flow of energy.

II. Embracing the Moon

This is for those with a good foundation of qi acquired through practice of the Horse Stance Posture, when the qi is strong enough to feed back to the body and influence the qi in the channels.

Practise the Swinging Arms Exercise for two minutes. Continue with the Horse Stance Posture for five minutes to build up qi for the following exercise. Follow the whole procedure of creating the Horse Stance Posture step by step from the beginning to the final posture, but remain in the posture for only 5 minutes. (This also applies to the other procedures from Fostering Primordial Qi to Regulating Qi Through Three Entry Points.)

1. Start in the Horse Stance Posture (Fig. 2.1).
2. Cross forearms in front of the body with the right hand over the left hand (Fig. 2.2). Move the forearms toward the body and place them parallel to the body and to each other, 2 inches (5 cm) apart with the right one on top. The top forearm should be at shoulder level. The tip of the middle finger is placed one inch ($2^1/_2$ cm) above the lower elbow Quchi LI11 point. The lower middle finger should be below the right elbow Quchi LI11 point (Fig. 2.3).
3. Extend the fingers of both hands. Hold the posture for a few seconds, then back to lady hand style for a few seconds. Repeat three times with opened and closed fingers.
4. Lower the elbows (Fig. 2.4). Make a cross with both hands, with right hand in front (Figs. 2.5 and 2.6). The palms should face the body, 2 inches (5 cm) away. The right hand overlaps the left hand, one inch ($2^1/_2$ cm) apart with the base of the thumbs lined up. Both Yuji L10 points of the palms point directly to Shanzhong C17, which is situated between the nipples. Hold for one minute.
5. Move the hands forward about 6 to 9 inches (15 to 23 cm) from the chest. Keep the hands in the same posture (Fig. 2.7). Hold for 30 seconds.
6. Return the hands to the position shown in Fig. 2.6. Hold for one minute.
7. Using your hands as a fulcrum, draw the elbows in and push the hands up to the front of the nose (Fig. 2.8) with Yuji L10 points of both hands pointing at the tip of the nose and the Laogong P8 points of both hands directed at Yingsiang LI20 (Fig. 2.9). Hold for one minute.
8. Bring the hands down to their earlier position over Shanzhong C17 (Fig. 2.5). Separate the hands and draw them sideways until the fingertips rest over the centre of the chest half an inch (1 cm) from the central line with fingers pointing at each other (Fig. 2.10). Move them down along the Conception meridian to rest over Zhongwan C12 halfway between the umbilicus and the lower end of the breastbone (Fig. 2.11). Hold for half a minute.
9. Bring the hands down and forward and move the forearms sideways to resume the Horse Stance Posture (Fig. 2.12). Hold for one minute.
10. Repeat the procedure from 2 to 8 above, this time with the left hand on top.
11. Complete with the Winding Up Procedure.

2.1
Horse
Stance
Posture.

2.4
Lower
elbows.

2.2
Cross
forearms.

2.5
Cross
hands
over
chest
2 inches
(5 cm)
away.

2.3
Bring
forearms
in with
fingers at
elbows.
Stretch
fingers
and then
relax
(3 times).

2.6
Side view
of 2.5.

2.7
Move hands forward to 6 inches (18 cm) from chest.

2.10
Draw elbows out, separating hands.

2.8
Bring hands up over nose.

2.11
Move hands down over Zhongwan C12 on abdomen.

2.9
Yuji L10 (base of thumb) and Laogong P8 (centre of palm).

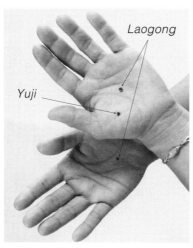

Laogong

Yuji

2.12
Return to Horse Stance Posture.

Total: 19 minutes.

Perform this exercise daily for 30 days or a total of 15 hours before going on to Fostering Primordial Qi.

Theory and Mechanism of Action

This posture features a special effect of Kong Jing Qigong called biofeedback. The qi produced and stored during the Horse Stance Posture is sent back to the body through the palms to set up a new balance of qi in the channels. To be effective, the qi acquired from the Horse Stance Posture must be strong. For this reason, you are advised to spend 20–30 minutes every day in the first few months doing the Horse Stance Posture, while proceeding with other postures at the same time.

Moving the palm from the hand to the forearm and elbow activates the three yin and the three yang channels of the hand. The fingering is to stimulate Shanzhong C17, giving a boost to the large intestine channel. The feedback at this point is of some importance, as Shanzhong C17 is the confluent point of all qi in the body. The activation of this point will also take care of the lungs and breast and treat bronchial asthma, cough, and inflammation of the breast.

For feedback of qi to the face, bring the palm Laogong P8 points to strike Yingsiang LI20 on the face. This will take care of rhinitis, sinusitis, nasal polyps, migraine, and facial itch.

The Yuji L10 point of the hand focuses on Suliao G25 of the Governor meridian at the tip of the nose. When the hands move down, they force the qi to bridge the gap between the end of the Governor meridian and the Conception meridian, on the upper and lower lips. This will drive the qi from the Governor meridian to flow down the Conception meridian, forming a closed circuit of circulation. This is the stage that the student of Qigong is aiming for. It will take some time to reach this level of accomplishment, but once it has been reached, the qi system will be geared to a higher level of performance. It will be able to bring the organs in the body to a new level of health and to raise the qi in the body to a new level for the self-treatment of disease.

Placing the tips of the middle fingers over Zhongwan C12 on the Conception meridian and the palms over the stomach channels on both sides will feed qi to these passages and regulate the gastrointestinal system. This movement of the hands over this region will relieve gastric pain, diarrhoea, vomiting, and abdominal distension.

III. Fostering Primordial Qi

Practise Swinging Arms Exercise for 2 minutes. Continue with Horse Stance Posture for 5 minutes. Start the exercise in the Horse Stance Posture (Fig. 3.1).

1. Open up the hands by stretching the fingers from the lady hand style (Fig. 3.2). Lift index fingers 20° (Fig. 3.3). Flex down 30° (Fig. 3.4). Hold for 45 seconds. Relax all fingers to lady hand style. Hold for 15 seconds.

NOTE: Always start by stretching the fingers before flexing individual fingers. After holding for 45 seconds, return to lady hand style for 15 seconds. The index finger is the only one that is lifted before bending.

2. Stretch fingers, then flex ring fingers down and hold for 45 seconds (Fig. 3.5). Go back to lady hand for 15 seconds.
3. Stretch fingers. Extend the thumbs sideways (Fig. 3.6), then bring them to below the index fingers (Fig. 3.7). Hold for 45 seconds. Go back to open fingers style, then lady hand style. Hold for 15 seconds.
4. Stretch fingers and flex little fingers down 30°. Hold for 45 seconds (Fig. 3.8). Go back to open fingers, then lady hand style. Hold for 15 seconds.
5. Stretch fingers. Flex middle finger down 30°. Hold for 45 seconds (Fig. 3.9). Go back to open fingers, then lady hand style. Hold for 15 seconds. The flexing of the five fingers constitutes one round. Continue for five rounds.
6. Stay in Horse Stance Posture for five minutes.
7. Perform Winding Up Procedure.

Total: 35 minutes.

Perform the exercise daily for 30 days (a total of 15 hours) before starting the next exercise.

Points to Note

1. All actions must be slow with muscles relaxed. Open fingers to their neutral position, taking care not to extend the fingers. The space between fingertips must not be more than $1/2$ inch (1 cm).
2. This is the only exercise where flexing of the finger is preceded by straightening out the fingers.
3. When flexing a finger, do not pull down an adjoining finger. If it does happen, do not bend the fingers too much at the beginning. About 15–20° will be all right. When you have mastered the movement, it can be increased to 30–40°.
4. The flexing sequence must be strictly followed: index finger, ring finger, thumb, little finger, middle finger.
5. If the proper sequence of the exercise is disrupted, just hold the fingers in a fist for 10 seconds, and start the whole exercise over with the index finger.
6. During the exercise, if you feel dizzy or cold, just do the Winding Up Procedure, rest a while, and take a warm drink. You will soon be all right, but wait eight hours before resuming exercise. Try to discover the cause of such problems— you may be too hungry or too full, sick, exhausted, or are exercising immediately after physical exercise or games. Refer to page 84.

3.1 Lady hand style.

3.2 Stretch out fingers.

3.3 Lift index fingers. Index fingers are the only ones lifted before flexing.

3.4 Flex index fingers. Hold for 45 seconds then return to lady hand style.

3.5 Stretch fingers, flex ring fingers, and hold for 45 seconds.

3.6 Stretch fingers. Extend thumbs to side.

3.8 Stretch fingers, flex little fingers, and hold.

3.7 Flex thumbs to below index fingers. Hold.

3.9 Stretch fingers, flex middle fingers, and hold.

Theory and Mechanism of Action

Fingering is another special feature of Kong Jing Qigong. It uses the flexing of the fingers to regulate qi circulation, instead of involving the whole body and limbs in intensive movement. Each of the six channels in the upper limbs runs to one of the five fingers, the little finger receiving two channels. By flexing each finger, the qi in its related channel is adjusted and any sickness in the associated organ is relieved.

The six channels of the foot are joined with the six channels of the hand in an internal-external relationship called coupling. The pairing can be seen as follows:

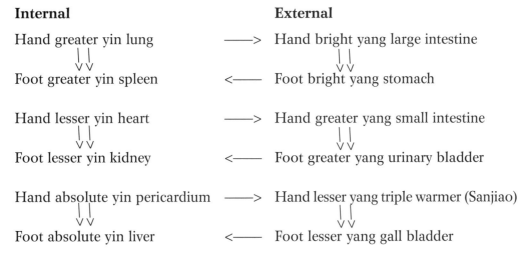

Internal	External
Hand greater yin lung ——>	Hand bright yang large intestine
Foot greater yin spleen <——	Foot bright yang stomach
Hand lesser yin heart ——>	Hand greater yang small intestine
Foot lesser yin kidney <——	Foot greater yang urinary bladder
Hand absolute yin pericardium ——>	Hand lesser yang triple warmer (Sanjiao)
Foot absolute yin liver <——	Foot lesser yang gall bladder

The coupling can be formed in two ways: internal and external coupling, yin and yang relation, indicated by a single arrow; and coupling by the same degree of polarity, indicated by double arrows.

This coupling of the energy channels is of great significance in the treatment of disease. Through the coupling relationship, regulation of one channel can also balance the other channel of the pair. For example, regulation of the lung channel can treat diseases of the lung as well as the large intestine channel through their yin and yang, or internal and external relation. Adjustments to the heart channel can treat diseases of the small intestine in addition to those of the heart. Couples of the same polarity are situated one on the foot and the other on the hand, such as the heart and kidney channels. Flexion of the fingers is held for 45 seconds for the qi to run down from the fingers to the toes and treat the coupled channel.

The five fingers of the hand have another special function in relation to the whole body, from the top down to the foot. The thumb controls mainly the head. The index finger controls the region from the collarbone down to the diaphragm. The middle finger takes charge of the area from the diaphragm to the umbilical region. The ring finger controls the area from the umbilicus to the pubic region. The little finger controls the area from the thigh downward.

Very often, when the region of the body controlled by a particular channel or the organ named after the channel is sick, the same acupuncture point on different sides of the body may show different electrical resistances. For example, Quchi LI11 on an unhealthy right elbow will show a high resistance when compared to the left Quchi point. When the sickness is cured, either by acupuncture or Qigong, the difference in the electrical resistance will be equalised. This indicates a balance of qi in the channels on both sides of the body.

IV. Holding the Ball With Both Hands

Practise Swinging Arms exercise for 2 minutes. Continue with Horse Stance Posture for 5 minutes. Begin the Holding the Ball With Both Hands exercise from the Horse Stance Posture (Fig. 4.1).

1. Cross the forearms in front of the body, with the right forearm on top, right Neiguan P6 above left Waiguan TW5 point, one inch ($2^1/_2$ cm) apart (Fig. 4.2).
2. Remaining in the above posture, turn the palms up (Fig. 4.3).
3. Open the elbows, bringing the hands to the centre of the body, right palm on top of left, both facing up. Turn the right palm down, palms facing each other 4 inches (10 cm) apart and 2 inches (5 cm) in front of the body, with the top hand at the level of Zhongwan C12 and the lower hand at the level of the umbilicus (Fig. 4.4). Hold for one minute.
4. Separate the palms. Bring the right hand up to Tiantu C22, in front of the breastbone, the left hand down to Guanyuan C4, midway between the umbilicus and the pubic bone (Fig. 4.5). Hold for 3 minutes. This will bring the heart yang qi from the chest down to communicate with the kidney yin qi rising from the abdomen.
5. Bring the hands closer again (Fig. 4.4). Hold for one minute.
6. Repeat step 4, separating the hands vertically (Fig. 4.5). Hold for 3 minutes.
7. Bring hands closer once again, as in step 5 (Fig. 4.4). Hold for one minute.
8. Repeat step 4, separating the hands vertically (Fig. 4.5). Hold for 3 minutes.
9. Bring hands close, as if holding a ball, and push away from the body (Fig. 4.6).
10. Separate the hands sideways (Fig. 4.7). Turn left palm down, returning to the Horse Stance Posture (Fig. 4.8). Hold for one minute.
11. Repeat 1 to 10 above, but with the left hand above and the right hand below.
12. Stay in the Horse Stance Posture for 5 minutes.
13. Complete Winding Up Procedure. The whole movement must be completed by winding up to bring the circulating qi to the elixir field to be stored.

The above procedure is a preparatory movement for the complete Holding the Ball exercise With Fingering, which requires one to be able to hold the hands in a vertically separated fashion for 10 minutes. The entire procedure includes the above movement with the addition of fingering only.

4.1
Horse
Stance
Posture.

4.3
Turn the
palms up.

4.2
Cross
forearms
in front.

4.4
Turn right
palm
down and
separate
arms
(holding
the ball
position).

Neiguan
P6 and
Waiguan
TW5
points.

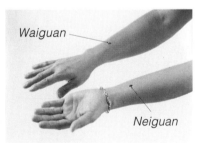

Waiguan

Neiguan

4.5
Move
hands
farther
apart.

4.7
Separate
hands,
moving
to sides.

4.6
Bring
hands
closer and
move
them
forward.

4.8
Turn left
palm
down to
return to
Horse
Stance.

V. *Holding the Ball With Fingering*

Practise Swinging Arms Exercise for 2 minutes. Continue with Horse Stance Posture for 5 minutes. Start Holding the Ball exercise at Horse Stance Posture (Fig. 4.1).

1. Cross forearms in front (Fig. 4.2).
2. Turn palms face up (Fig. 4.4)
3. Move hands to holding ball position, right hand on top (Fig. 4.5). Hold for one minute.
4. Move hands farther apart (Fig. 4.6). Start fingering with top (right) hand, leaving the bottom (left) hand still.
    a) Bend the thumb, middle finger, and ring finger of the right hand only 40°, with the thumb below the index finger (Figs. 5.1 and 5.2). Hold for 45 seconds. Then go back to normal, or lady hand style, for 15 seconds.
    b) Bend thumb and little finger for 45 seconds (Fig. 5.3). Then return to lady hand style for 15 seconds.
    c) Bend thumb and index finger and hold for 45 seconds (Fig. 5.4). Then return to lady hand style for 15 seconds.
    d) Bend thumb and middle finger for 45 seconds (Fig. 5.5). Then return to lady hand style for 15 seconds.
    e) Bend thumb, index finger, and ring finger for 45 seconds (Fig. 5.6). Return to normal for 15 seconds.

Always bring the bent finger back to lady hand style before the next fingering step. Adjust the wrist to let the bent fingers point at the palm of the hand opposite.

5. Now use the lower (left) hand to continue fingering, holding the top right hand still. Without changing posture, flex the fingers of the left hand as follows:
    a) Thumb, middle finger, and ring finger for 45 seconds (Fig. 5.7). Return to lady hand style for 15 seconds.
    b) Thumb and little finger for 45 seconds (Fig. 5.8). Return to lady hand style for 15 seconds.
    c) Thumb and index finger for 45 seconds (Fig. 5.9). Return to lady hand style for 15 seconds.
    d) Thumb and middle finger for 45 seconds (Fig. 5.10). Return to lady hand style for 15 seconds.
    e) Thumb, index finger, and ring finger for 45 seconds (Fig. 5.11). Return to lady hand style for 15 seconds.
6. Bring hands closer. Push the imaginary ball forward (Fig. 4.7). Separate the hands sideways to return to the Horse Stance Posture with hands facing down (Fig. 4.9). Hold for one minute.
7. Repeat the procedure, but with the left hand on top. Repeat fingering first with the top (left) hand, followed by the lower (right) hand.
8. End with the Horse Stance Posture, holding for 5 minutes.
9. Complete Winding Up Procedure.

Total: 30 minutes.

5.1
Flex thumb, middle finger, and ring finger of right hand and hold for 45 seconds.

5.2
Closeup of 5.1.

5.4
Flex thumb and index finger.

5.3
Flex thumb and little finger.

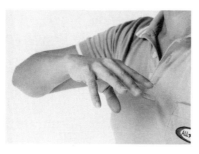

5.5
Flex thumb and middle finger.

5.6
Flex thumb, index finger, and ring finger.

5.7
*Flex
thumb,
middle
finger, and
ring finger
of left
hand.*

5.10
*Flex thumb
and middle
finger.*

5.8
*Flex thumb
and little
finger.*

5.11
*Flex
thumb,
index
finger, and
ring finger.*

5.9
*Flex thumb
and index
finger.*

Practise Holding the Ball With Fingering every day for 30 days and complete the whole course for a total of 15 hours before going on to the Rolling the Ball Exercise.

Points to Note

- Laogong P8 point at the centre of the palms should be aligned vertically all the time while fingering.
- Up and down movement of the hands should follow the Conception meridian in the centre of the body. Hands are held about 2 inches (5 cm) from the body.
- Flex the finger at the phalange metacarpal joint, the third joint from the fingertip. Flexing is done in lady hand style without straightening first. Bend fingers 30° or 40° only, to point at the palm of the hand opposite.
- The shoulders must be dropped and relaxed.
- The whole procedure must be completed in one session. If for some reason it is only partially completed, the other part should be finished later to allow the qi to circulate in balance.

Theory and Mechanism of Action

Crossing the forearms stimulates communication between Neiguan P6 of the hand absolute yin pericardium channel and Yinwei Mai (meridian), and between Waiguan TW5 of the hand lesser yang triple warmer (Sanjiao) channel and the Yangwei Mai. The Yangwei Mai communicates with all the yang channels, and the Yinwei Mai with all the yin channels in the body. The Yinwei Mai also meets the Conception meridian at Tiantu C22 point over the top of the breastbone. Normally, the Yinwei Mai and Yangwei Mai are not involved in qi and blood circulation. Their functions are mainly to keep the yin and yang channels in balance.

From electrical studies, it has been found that the channels can receive electromagnetic messages. Messages sent from the nervous system are in the form of electrical impulses, and the channels are able to use this electrical transmission to influence their qi and thus change its circulation. The electromagnetic field in the palm is stronger than in any other part of the body. The palm can send this energy and infrared radiation to stimulate yang qi in the body and heart to get rid of any stagnation in blood flow. This is accomplished by the palms in the Holding the Ball procedure. The lower hand, which faces upward, sends qi from Laogong P8 point to induce the yang qi to stimulate the heart. The upper hand, which faces down, sends qi from Laogong P8 to stimulate qi flow in the blood vessels. The opening and closing of the palms in an up-and-down movement further enhances the force of qi circulation. The Holding the Ball procedure is therefore beneficial to the heart, especially helping in diseases associated with coronary insufficiency due to narrowing of the coronary artery, leading to cardiac failure.

Fingering is also beneficial to the triple warmer (Sanjiao) channel. Laogong P8 point on the palm belongs to the pericardium channel, which is connected to the triple warmer channel. The triple warmer channel involves the pericardial pleural cavity and the peritoneal cavity, which embrace all organs in the body except the brain and the testes. It is a very important channel as it controls all qi function in the body, embracing the elixir field of the qi "battery" and controlling changes produced by the movement of qi. It also governs qi transformation, which includes the metabolism of matter and the transformation of energy from external sources for use as energy. It plays an important part in strengthening the circulation of internal qi for emission to another person in qi therapy as external qi. By bringing the two Laogong P8 to face each other, it is possible to strengthen the pericardium channel and enhance the functioning of the triple warmer channel from their inner and external or yin and yang relationship. The bending of the fingers directed at Laogong P8 is to exchange internal qi in the various channels present in the fingers with qi in the triple warmer channel, thus increasing qi circulation. The channels in the fingers are:

Thumb: lung channel

Index finger: large intestine channel

Middle finger: pericardium channel

Ring finger: triple warmer (Sanjiao) channel

Little finger: heart and small intestine channel

Qi from the palms also influences other organs. The hands are held with the upper palm facing down at the top of the breastbone, and the lower palm facing up at the level of the lower abdomen. The qi field between them covers the important points along the Conception meridian, which are connected above the umbilicus to the channels of the gastrointestinal system, and below the umbilicus to the genital organs and the kidneys. The qi field from the hands strengthens these organs and helps prevent and treat disease there.

VI. Rolling the Ball

Practise Swinging Arms Exercise for 2 minutes. Continue with the Horse Stance Posture for 5 minutes. Start with the Rolling Ball exercise without fingering (as it is difficult for beginners to do this exercise right away, especially the side rolling).

1. Begin with the Horse Stance Posture (Fig. 6.1). Bring both hands to the right waist. Form a triangle with the thumbs and index fingers (Fig. 6.2).
2. Lift the left toes. Turn your body to the left, pivoting on the left heel. Put down toes, forming a 90° angle with the right foot (Fig. 6.3). Bend the knees with the body facing toward the left toes. Roll both hands slowly from right waist in a circle, curving out in front and then drawing back to the left waist. Both palms should be facing the body at a 45° angle (Figs. 6.4 and 6.5). Draw the hands from the left waist across the abdomen to the right waist to complete the circle. The palms should be facing the ground (Fig. 6.6). Repeat this movement 20 times at 8 rounds per minute. Finish with both hands resting at the left waist.
3. Turn your body to the front with the left foot facing the front (Fig. 6.7). Turn the right foot to the right with the body, making a 90° angle to the left foot (Fig. 6.8). Bring both hands from the left waist to curve out in front and roll to the right waist (Figs. 6.9 and 6.10). Bring both hands back from the right waist to the left in front of the abdomen to complete one circle (Fig. 6.11). Roll 20 times in $2^1/2$ minutes. Finish with both hands resting at the right waist.
4. Turn your body and right foot to the front to return to the Horse Stance Posture. Bring hands from the right waist, stretching the arms to make a curve in front of the body from the right to the left, ending at the left waist (Figs. 6.12 and 6.13). Lay both hands flat to face the ground and bring them across the abdomen, 2 inches (5 cm) from the body, to the right waist to complete one round. Roll 20 times from right to left, counterclockwise, in $2^1/2$ minutes, finishing with hands at the left waist.
5. Roll 20 times clockwise in $2^1/2$ minutes, starting from left waist, with the same movement as above. Finish with both hands resting in the centre (Fig. 6.14).
6. Push hands out to form the Horse Stance Posture and hold for 5 minutes.
7. Complete Winding Up Procedure.

Slowly increase the rolling movement day by day until you can roll the hands 40 times on one side. You are then ready to start Rolling the Ball With Fingering.

Points to Note

- Movements should be slow, smooth, continuous, and relaxed.
- When rolling to the side, the body should face the direction of the front foot, remaining in place without following the rolling hands.
- The rolling movement is like sliding the palms over the top edge of a big ball and forming a 45° angle with the ground. The hands should be 2 inches (5 cm) away from the abdomen.
- The hands should keep the triangle shape, whatever position they assume.

6.1
Horse
Stance
Posture.

6.4
Roll hands
to left,
making a
wide
curve in
front.

6.2
Bring
hands to
right
waist,
forming a
triangle
with
thumbs
and index
fingers.

6.5
Hands
stop at
left waist.

6.3
Turn body
to the
left,
pivoting
on left
heel.

6.6
Roll hands back to the right, palms facing down. Roll 20 times, ending with hands at left.

6.9
Roll hands to the right, making a wide curve in front.

6.7
Turn body to face front.

6.10
Hands stop at right waist.

6.8
Turn body to the right, pivoting on right heel.

6.11
Roll hands
back to
left,
palms
facing
down.
Roll 20
times,
ending
with
hands at
right.

6.13
Roll 20
times.
Hands
end at
left waist.
Roll 20
times in
opposite
direction.

6.12
Turn body
to face
front.
Roll hands
to left,
then back
to right,
forming a
full circle.

6.14
Hands end
at centre
front.

VII. Rolling the Ball With Fingering

Rolling the Ball is a preparatory training procedure that upgrades to the Rolling the Ball With Fingering exercise once you can do the rolling movement 40 times in each phase. There are five sets of fingering. Each set of fingering must roll 8 times. The five sets will take a total of 40 rounds to complete and 5 minutes for each phase (the left side, right side, and the two front phases).

Procedure

Practise the Swinging Arms Exercise for 2 minutes. Continue with the Horse Stance Posture for 5 minutes.

1. From the Horse Stance Posture, bring the hands to the right waist (Figs. 6.1, 6.2, and 6.3).
2. With the body turned to the left, you will start to roll from the right waist to the left, bending the fingers as indicated. Bend the ring fingers and roll 8 rounds (Fig. 7.1). Bend the index fingers and roll 8 rounds (Fig. 7.2). Bend the little fingers and roll 8 rounds (Fig. 7.3). Bend the middle fingers and roll 8 rounds (Fig. 7.4). Bend thumbs and ring fingers together and roll 8 rounds (Fig. 7.5). Total: 5 minutes.
3. Repeat the same sequence of fingering (ring fingers, index fingers, little fingers, middle fingers, thumbs and ring fingers), with the body turned to the right.
4. Repeat the same fingering with the body in front, counterclockwise first for 40 rounds (each finger 8 rounds). Total: 5 minutes.
5. Repeat the same sequence of fingering in a clockwise direction, 8 rounds each. Total: 5 minutes.
6. Continue with the Horse Stance Posture for 5 minutes.
7. Complete the Winding Up Procedure.

The four phases of rolling with fingering take 20 minutes. Including both initial and final Horse Stance Posture, the total time is 30 minutes. Do the Rolling the Ball With Fingering exercise every day for 30 days to complete the course of 15 hours before proceeding to Regulating Qi Through Three Entry Points.

Points to Follow

- Bend the finger at the third joint from the fingertip at a 30–40° angle.
- Bend fingers direct from lady hand style. Do not straighten before bending.
- The weight of the body falls more on the back leg when rolling on the side.
- Both knees should be bent. The back knee should bend more when side rolling.
- Slightly bend the elbow when in the rolling motion, to make sure the triangle formed by the hands is maintained and the arm is relaxed.
- Do not allow the body to follow the hands when rolling. Keep the body still and relaxed. Just let the arms do the movements.

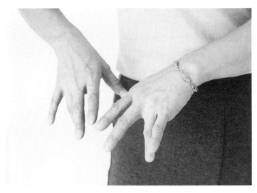

7.1 Flex ring fingers and roll 8 times.

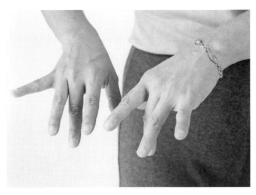

7.4 Flex middle fingers.

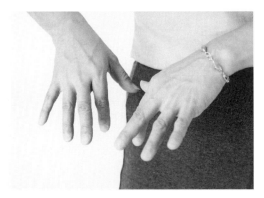

7.2 Flex index fingers.

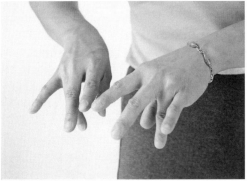

7.5 Flex thumbs and ring fingers.

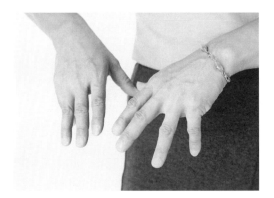

7.3 Flex little fingers.

Theory and Mechanism of Action

The hands carry a large amount of electromagnetism in Qigong exercise. This energy, when emitted to any part of the body, whether in feedback action to oneself or to another person, influences the circulation of energy in the channels. In the rolling movement, the hands with their strong electromagnetic field stimulate the Belt and Conception meridians. The Belt meridian enhances the qi of the six yin channels. The Conception meridian follows the short cut through the Belt meridian to control the six yin channels more efficiently. The rolling movement sweeps over the abdominal organs, including the liver, spleen, stomach, gall bladder and kidneys, and the genital organs, to directly influence their electromagnetic field. Fingering increases feedback of qi to the channels and meridians, producing a therapeutic effect in the organs. It is particularly effective for swelling in the abdomen.

The rolling movement boosts production of B- and T-lymphocyte and immune globulin. During the side rolling movement, the qi flows from the back leg to the front leg due to the lessening of tension in the front leg muscles. The fingering further increases feedback qi entering the six channels of the lower limbs. This is particularly beneficial for diseases of the lower limb joints.

With this exercise, the pulsating force becomes very powerful, and blood and qi circulation increases. The exchange of internal and environmental external qi is continuously enhanced. Qi circulation in the body depends mainly on the 12 main channels. Regulation of qi circulation falls on the Governor, Conception, and Belt meridians. The Belt meridian plays a very important role. Once the Belt meridian is activated, it brings the Governor and Conception meridians into action. The 12 channels then follow suit.

VIII. Regulating Qi Through Three Entry Points

Practise Swinging Arms Exercise for 2 minutes. Continue with the Horse Stance Posture for 5 minutes. Begin with the Horse Stance Posture (Fig. 8.1).

1. Turn the right palm to face the left hand (Fig. 8.2). Move the right palm toward the left hand slowly for 8 seconds. Hold the right palm with the right Laogong P8 pointing to the left Hegu LI4, 3 inches (8 cm) away, for 10 seconds (Figs. 8.3 and 8.4).

2. Bring your right palm down to below your left palm to face each other with tips of middle fingers pointing at each other's Zhongchong P9 (Fig. 8.5). The tip of the right middle finger traces the midline of your left hand and forearm to below the left elbow, following the pericardium channel (Fig. 8.6). With your right palm facing up, bring it from the left across the front of your abdomen to your right side (Fig. 8.7). Bring your right elbow to the side at shoulder level, turning your right hand with palm facing away from the body (Fig. 8.8).

3. Bring both hands to the centre of your body, right Hegu LI4 in front of the chin, facing Laogong P8 point of left hand below (Fig. 8.9). Bring down the right elbow, turning the right palm down to face the left palm, keeping them 6 inches (15 cm) apart (Fig. 8.10). Hold for 30 seconds.

4. Separate the hands, moving the right hand up to the right side of your head and the left hand outside the hip joint. Keep the palms facing each other (Fig. 8.11). Hold for 3 minutes. Bend your right ring finger to point at your left Laogong P8 (Fig. 8.12). Hold for 30 seconds and then return to normal. Bend your left ring finger to point at your right Laogong P8 (Fig. 8.13). Hold for 30 seconds and then return to normal. Bend both right and left ring fingers to point at each other for one minute (Fig. 8.14). Return to normal.

5. Bring hands together, meeting in front. Turn your left palm down. Your right hand approaches the left hand, right palm directed at the tip of your left ring finger, Guanchong TW1 point (Fig. 8.15). Move your right palm up to your left elbow, following the triple warmer (Sanjiao) channel (Fig. 8.16). Continue movement up your left arm to the shoulder (Fig. 8.17). From your left shoulder move your right palm over the upper chest to the right (Fig. 8.18). Move your right palm down the right nipple line longitudinally to the abdomen (Fig. 8.19). Bring both hands out to form the Horse Stance Posture. Hold for one minute.

6. Repeat the exercise as above, but starting with the left hand.

7. Stay in the Horse Stance Posture for 5 minutes.

8. Complete the Winding Up Procedure.

Perform this movement daily for 30 days, or 15 hours.

Points to be Observed

- The three points of entry are Hegu LI4 of the large intestine channel, Zhongchong P9 of the pericardium channel, and Guanchong TW1 of the triple warmer (Sanjiao) channel.

- Movements 2 to 3 are the hardest to perform. They include raising the elbow and turning the wrist and the palm. The movements are designed to send out qi from the lower Laogong P8 to Hegu LI4 on top. Therefore, during these movements, your lower palm must follow the upper palm all the way up.

- Your elbow should not be higher than your shoulder. The raised elbow should stay still to allow your forearm to rise to elbow level. The raised hand is brought to below your chin with Hegu LI4 pointing down to the lower palm.

- When flexing your ring finger, bend the second phalangeal joint, so that the tip of the ring finger can easily point to Laogong P8. Slight bending of your wrist is allowed to facilitate this movement.

- In all these movements, your shoulders must stay relaxed and dropped.

- It is important, before practising this procedure, that you first practise Arms Embracing the Moon, Holding the Ball, and Rolling the Ball procedures for some time so that the qi will be strong enough to be emitted as external qi and exert its influence. Otherwise the results will not be good.

- It is better to practise Regulating Qi Through Three Entry Points with a greater degree of knee bending so that the lower hand will be at the lateral side of the knee.

8.1
Horse
Stance
Posture.

8.4
Hegu LI4
on left
hand and
Laogong
P8 on
right
palm.

Laogong

Hegu

8.5
Bring
right hand
down and
turn palm
up
to pass
below left
hand.

8.2
Turn right
palm to
face left
hand,
so that
Laogong
P8 points
to Hegu
LI4.

8.6
Right
hand
traces
pericar-
dium
channel
up left
arm.

8.3
Bring
right hand
toward
left.

8.7
Bring right hand across in front of abdomen.

8.10
Bring right palm down to face left in rolling the ball position. Hold 30 seconds.

8.8
Bring right hand up above shoulder with palm facing away.

8.11
Separate hands on a diagonal with palms facing each other. Hold 3 minutes.

8.9
Bring hands back to centre of body with right Hegu LI4 pointed at left Laogong P8.

8.12
Flex right ring finger to point at left palm. Hold 30 seconds.

8.14
Flex both ring fingers. Hold one minute.

8.13
Flex left ring finger.

8.15
Bring hands down to centre with palms down.

8.16
Right
palm
follows
triple
warmer
channel
up left
arm.

8.18
Bring right
hand across
chest and
left hand
out to side.

8.17
Right
hand ends
at shoul-
der.

8.19
Bring right
hand down
to abdomen
and resume
Horse
Stance
Posture.
Hold one
minute.

Theory and Mechanism of Action

This movement aims to regulate the three yin and the three yang channels of the upper limbs. It is used to increase the exchange of internal and external qi. It enhances the Belt meridian, thereby improving energy circulation in the Governor and Conception meridians and the 12 main channels. It is beneficial for diseases of the spleen, liver, and digestive system. Fingering with the ring finger is performed to train it to send qi through the fingertips. The pointing of Laogong P8 is done to prevent wastage of the emitted qi. The exchange of qi from one palm to the other is used to help you feel the presence of qi.

Now that you have completed the above procedures, you can choose to do any procedure you please, or select one that is beneficial to a particular illness. For example, Arms Embracing the Moon is especially good for sinusitis, migraine, and bronchitis. Holding the Ball With Fingering is particularly suited for heart and lung diseases.

Chapter 7

Healing with Qigong: Some Case Studies

This is the most important and interesting section of the book. It is the result of my 10-year study on Qigong exercise in the treatment of chronic diseases that modern medicine has difficulty managing.

The medical treatment for migraine is only symptomatic – it suppresses the headaches temporarily, and recurrence is frequent. Some drugs have been tried as a prophylactic measure, i.e., to ward off the disease, or to lessen the pain in future attacks. These, however, have failed to achieve their purpose. Some other medications produce very adverse side effects, such as the forming of fibrosis around blood vessels and the constriction of blood flow. Operations are then needed to relieve the blockage.

Some cases of chronic sinusitis have been operated on either to drain off the accumulating fluid in the maxillary sinus (the air cavity in the cheekbone which connects to the nose) or to remove the polyp (a smooth rounded growth from the mucous membrane of the sinus). Modern medications, especially antibiotics, have been able to control infection well. But the allergic element is hard to eliminate. The inflammatory fluids will eventually infiltrate again and the polyps will grow again.

Chronic Fatigue Syndrome (CFS) and Fibromyalgia Syndrome (FMS) are probably the most serious chronic diseases. In the past 10 years, the American Center for Disease Control (CDC) has sponsored millions of dollars for research on them. Yet the causes of CFS and FMS are still not definitely known, while hypotheses are numerous. Medical treatment for these two diseases continues to be a total failure. With CFS cases, disturbed sleep is an uncontrollable problem. The extreme exhaustion after physical exertion in CFS cases is hard to manage.

The muscular pain experienced by FMS cases is very persistent, despite the administering of strong analgesics or painkillers.

Case 1

I have been teaching people Qigong exercise to improve their health twice weekly since 1990. In that first year, I had a student with a 30-year history of chronic sinusitis. All those years she had received palliative treatment to alleviate the problem without getting cured. It was not easy to convince her to take up this Qigong.

Eventually, when the sinusitis developed into bronchial asthma, she was prompted to join the class. The asthma had persisted for six months, even with medication. She had no choice but to take up the exercise, albeit without much confidence. Within a few months, the asthma became controlled and so did her 30-year-old condition of chronic sinusitis (see case studies). She was delighted to be rid of her plague and has since continued to exercise daily.

As for me, I was more then overjoyed. As a medical practitioner, I have handled many cases of chronic sinusitis. I treated the condition using both modern medicine and antibiotics. At times I had to use acupuncture with antibiotics when the patients' condition worsened. All measures taken seemed to be merely palliative. The patients had to come back from time to time. However, Qigong achieves impressive results in the treatment of these diseases as it clears the sinusitis completely and with ease. The results became so encouraging that I soon embarked on a study of the healing effects of Qigong on other diseases as well.

Case 2

I had the first case of Chronic Fatigue Syndrome (CFS) in 1992. She was a Taiwanese who had suffered from CFS for more than 20 years since her teenage years. All kinds of tests were carried out (see case studies). She was then diagnosed with anemia and general weakness, as at that time little was known of CFS.

Modern medicine did not help much, so she sought herbal treatments and reflexology. Kong Jing Qigong, which I had chosen to teach her to combat her illness, focuses on the building up of energy (qi). This is done through posturing. The regulating of the qi within is carried out by flexing the fingers and executing some postures together. I consider that merely regulating the energy (qi) is of little value if the energy itself is lacking.

Within a few months, she had regained her health. She felt as if she had been reborn. Realizing that Qigong exercise was very effective, she practised it for four hours a day (two hours in the morning and two hours in the evening). One year later, she went overseas on a sightseeing trip. She was so healthy that she was able to outrun a friend. She was thus convinced that this form of exercise was beneficial.

After her second year of practising Qigong, she returned to Taiwan. She was able to give out qi from her palm to relieve her mother's arthritis pain. It is noted that a person with more than five years of Qigong practice is strong enough to give out qi to treat patients for certain diseases.

Case 3

The second case of CFS came to me in 1993. She is a successful professional. The diagnosis was made through exclusion after extensive investigation (including blood test, scanning, and X-rays) proved negative. She had received medical treatment for one year without improvement in her condition.

After quite some time, she became more depressed and tired easily, even without any physical exertion. She refused to move or mix with people. Four good friends were anxious to help her and accompanied her to Qigong sessions. I could see that she was trying to be brave and struggled to do the exercises so as not to let her friends down.

The rewards came soon after one month of practice. She could sleep much better. Then came other improvements. Her appetite became better and her body grew stronger. After a few months, she was able to resume full-time work.

Even the Samaritans who had accompanied her to Qigong class reaped some benefits. Two who had moderate migraines in the past found their attacks receding steadily, and within a few months were rid of the problem.

Case 4

I encountered a severe case of migraine in 1994. The patient had the full-blown clinical features of severe migraine with the typical aura of a classic migraine (see case studies). Her migraines had become so bad that she was forced to apply for a year of unpaid sick leave to rest. At the beginning, she had to take painkillers to practise Qigong. After two months, she was able to cast off the drugs altogether. She continued to do Qigong for about one year, and stopped as she was perfectly normal again. When I enquired about her headaches four years later, she told me that she had completely forgotten about the migraines.

Throughout the years, I have continued my research on the healing effect of Qigong on various other chronic diseases. I have had experience with cases of Ménière's disease, Rheumatoid Arthritis, Lower Backache and Sciatica, Systemic Lupus Erythromatosis (SLE), Anxiety, Panic Disorder, Depression, Resistant Hypertension, Asthma, Cardiac Failure, and Icthyosis (characterized by dry and scaly skin). I have had good results with all of them.

At the moment I find Fibromyalgia Syndrome (FMS) and SLE most challenging. Medical treatment proves ineffective for FMS, which has similar clinical features to CFS, and both manifest dysfunction of the brain. SLE stands out because of its prevalence and its involvement of multiple organs.

After 10 years of study and follow-up, I have become completely convinced of the healing effect of Qigong in some chronic diseases. I consider a disease cured if the patient is feeling well with no recurrence for more than five years, as in the cases of CFS, Migraine and Chronic Sinusitis. I am very satisfied with the results and wish very much to share them with the people who are suffering from these chronic diseases and are searching for remedies. I have compiled this book with many illustrations and a video compact disc to facilitate self-learning. The exercises are very easy to learn and will not cause ill effects when followed correctly.

For your better understanding, I have presented the case studies of the various chronic diseases in the following pages for your reference.

Case Studies

A. *Chronic Fatigue Syndrome*

Fatigue is one of the most common symptoms of diseases seen in clinical practice. It can present in almost all the human illnesses, be they organic or psychological, and also in normal physical exertion. In the majority of cases, fatigue will resolve once the patient is cured of the disease. Fatigue due to physical exertion will disappear after rest.

However, Chronic Fatigue Syndrome is chronic and relapsing fatigue of a profound, generalized nature, and persists for months or years. Its prevalence rate in the United States is quite high. Between September 1989 and September 1991, millions of people there were found to be suffering from this sickness. Incidence of CFS in the United States ranged from between 0.05 percent and 0.11 percent of the population aged 18 years and above, and 82 percent of the patients were female. The average age of onset was 30 years and the average duration of the illness at the time of the study was 7.1 years. Before the illness, the median energy level on a scale of 1 to 100 was 95. At the worst point in the illness, it was 12.

CFS has been recognized as a disease entity only in recent years, and the Center for Disease Control (CDC) of the United States has spent US$4 million to sponsor research on the disease. To meet the requirements for CFS diagnosis in a study, patients must have at least two of the physical criteria and at least six of the symptomatic criteria that follow:

a. Major physical criteria

1. The onset of persistent or relapsing, debilitating fatigue, severe enough to reduce or impair average daily activity below 50 percent of premorbid activity for a period of six or more months.
2. Exclusion of other causes by thorough evaluation based on clinical appraisal and appropriate laboratory findings.

b. Minor symptomatic criteria

1. Mild fever or chills.
2. Sore throat.
3. Painful lymph nodes on neck or armpit.
4. Unexplained generalized muscle weakness.
5. Muscular discomfort or pain.

6. Generalized fatigue lasting more than 24 hours and following a level of exercise that would have been easily tolerated in previous healthy state.
7. Generalized headaches different from those previously experienced.
8. Shifting pain, from joint to joint, without swelling or redness.
9. Neuropsychological complaints. One or more of the following: photophobia (fear of light, visual disturbance), forgetfulness, irritability, confusion, poor concentration, depression, and difficulty in thinking and memory loss.
10. Sleep disturbance, difficulty with sleep or oversleeping.
11. Rapid onset over hours.

Unfortunately, despite so many years of research, the causes of CFS are still not known. What has emerged from the research points to the dysfunction of the brain and the immune system.

The parts of the brain involved are the limbic system and the frontal lobe, with accompanying decrease in growth hormone and serotonin. The limbic system in the brain regulates the immune system as well as the memory, hormonal processes, pain, fatigue, sleep, and the action of the nervous system. The growth hormone aids in routine tissue repair and serotonin is involved in sleep regulation.

The best description of a case of CFS was written by a medical doctor who was suffering from the disease himself in 1994. He coined the term "myalgic encephalomyelitis" to replace CFS, as the disease involves the dysfunction of the brain and the muscle. He wrote the article in the third person, describing how the patient had to spend six frightening, frustrating months with no definite diagnosis since there was no objective test to confirm the sickness. He had to come to terms with the disease, as no treatment was known to be effective. The severity of the symptoms and the debilitation caused by CFS are often underestimated by the attending physician, family, and friends, and appear to be of a malingering nature.

Muscular weakness could be so great that the patient battled to carry his own weight. He could not maintain his grip on the steering wheel of his car for more than a few seconds. The exercised muscles started to contract for hours after use. (Most sufferers will confirm the presence of muscle aches, particularly at night.) This contributed to unrefreshing sleep, although he slept for nine to 10 hours every night.

The cerebral symptoms were severe, and he found these most difficult to contend with. They included poor memory for recent events, difficulty in concentrating, recurrent headaches, tinnitus (noises in the ear such as ringing, buzzing, or clicking), depression, hyperacusis (great sensitivity to noise), extreme sensitivity to movement, and a fuzzy sensation in the brain after concentrating for a long period or after exercise.

Traditional medicine did not help at all. He found social interaction tiring and loathed rapid movements of children and high-pitched sounds.

Case 1

The first case of CFS came to me in 1992. She had had the disease for 20 years since her teenage days. It was such a long time ago that she did not remember how it started. What she knew was that she was feeling weak and tired all the time. She tried to spend more time sleeping, hoping to regain her energy. Yet she had insomnia and disturbed dreams that left her as tired as before.

She had occasional abdominal pain with poor appetite. She could not take standard food and rice and had to go on a vegetarian diet. Moderate bodily exertion or concentration tired her easily. During her final examination at university, she had severe headaches and vomiting. She had to have a needle put into the arm to stop the headaches and vomiting in order to take the examination. She looked thin and pale and resorted to herbs and tonics to build up her health.

At one stage, it was suspected that she had a blood disease and a bone marrow puncture was done to take a blood sample for examination. Fortunately, no leukemia (a fatal disease with marked increase in white blood cells) was found. A series of tests followed which included blood and urine tests and X-rays. No abnormality was detected. She was diagnosed with anemia and general weakness; CFS was little known then. She received treatment but her condition remained the same.

She moved with her husband from Taiwan to Sarawak. Her energy level was about 50 out of 100. She had tried various remedies including Qigong exercise and reflexology with no improvement.

When she first attended my class, she was unusually thin and pale. Her hands were very white and cold. Cold hands in a patient always indicate a low energy level. I started her with the Horse Stance Posture (see Qigong exercise), which is mainly for building up qi. After about 10 minutes on the posture, I could feel the cold wave of air coming from her and passing through me. This was because as her energy was building, her negative energy (yin qi) had been flushed out from her body. Such negative energy is called aberrant qi.

In health, the positive and negative energy must be balanced. In sickness, the positive energy is suppressed and negative energy becomes stronger.

After a few sessions she began to sweat profusely after 10 minutes on the fixed Horse Stance Posture. It was as if she was playing badminton. This was due to the exercising of the organs in the body in contrast to physical exercise such as in a game, with a lot of bodily movement.

After two months, her cheeks started to become rosy and she looked very fresh. The hands were warm. She slept more soundly and her appetite improved. She experienced the rebound phenomenon after two months of practice. This came in the form of foot joint and finger pain, which lasted for about 10 days. It soon disappeared after continuing with exercise. All her complaints disappeared after one year. She became very healthy and active with no recurrence up to the year 2000.

Case 2

I started on the second case of CFS in 1993. She was a well-established professional, robust and previously active in sports and games. Starting in 1992, after a slight fever and sore throat, she began tire easily. The fatigue progressively worsened until she could not even drive her car. She struggled to work for half a day, but found it so exhausting that she had to take two days off. Her memory became impaired and her concentration power slackened. She had insomnia and loss of appetite, as well as nausea and vomiting. She had headaches and felt depressed.

Various tests were done including brain scans. No positive results were found. She was diagnosed with CFS by exclusion of other possible causes of fatigue. She received medication for depression, anxiety, and sleep disturbance. Tonics were given for one year, in an attempt to restore her energy and wakefulness. However, there were no signs of improvement.

She came to see me, looking pale and tired, with a pair of cold hands. Many Qigong exercises that involved a lot of bodily movement would not suit her, as the exertion would make her more fatigued. So I started her on the Horse Stance Posture, as with the first case. This posture would produce more positive qi.

The schedule I worked out for her (similar to the first case) was as follows:

Postures	Total Time
1. Horse Stance Posture	15 hours
2. Arms Embracing the Moon	15 hours
3. Fostering Primordial Qi	15 hours
4. Holding the Ball	15 hours
5. Rolling the Ball	15 hours
6. Regulating Qi Through Three Entry Points	15 hours

Her energy level at the time was about 30 points out of 100, compared with the first case. I had to prolong the Horse Stance Posture to 50 hours to restore her energy. In Chinese medicine, CFS is considered an illness due to deficiency of yang qi (the positive phase of the energy) and sluggish qi circulation. Because of this, the patient would get a yin disease. Someone with yin disease presents as one who is fatigued, depressed, and pale, is fond of quiet, has cold extremities, is short of breath, and is afraid of cold.

Kong Jing Qigong soon built up her yang qi, warmed her hands and gave colour to her cheeks. The first wonderful thing it brought her was sound, refreshing sleep one month after she began Qiqong. Sleep is important in tissue restoration and bodily renewal and in regulating the neuroendocrine and immune functions.

She did not feel the chill any more and was more energetic. She was able to concentrate better. She regained her memory. Her appetite came back. After four months, before completing the whole exercise schedule, she was able to resume work fully. She continued the exercise for a few more months, then stopped. The sickness has not recurred.

B. Chronic Sinusitis

Sinusitis is caused by the inflammation of the nose and the cavities in the face bone called the sinuses. Nasal cavities open the direct route of contact for the lungs to the outside environment. The nose continuously inhales air into the lungs for life sustaining oxygen in exchange for carbon dioxide, a waste product of the body. It is exposed constantly to all the insults of the air, which is laden with harmful materials, including pollen, smoke, virus, and bacteria. Sinusitis is therefore the most common complaint in medical practice. In the United States, it was estimated that more than 33 million people were suffering from sinusitis in 1993.

Incorrect diagnosis and treatment of sinusitis can lead to prevalent or chronic sinusitis. It could also lead to complications like eye and intracranial infections forming brain abscess by transmission of bacteria directly or through the blood.

Any factor that disturbs the nasal lining, cilia (hair-like process attached to the surface of the cell), will result in impaired ventilation or discharge of the nose, predisposing to sinusitis. This often presents as an inflammation of the sinus and it is most often due to infection. It can also be due to cigarette smoke, other inhaled substances, and environmental pollution.

Chronic sinusitis will develop if the natural opening of the sinus to the nose is blocked for a period of three to four weeks. The problem may drag on for six months, even with medical treatment.

The common signs of chronic sinusitis are discharge from the nose, nasal congestion or obstruction (blocked nose), absence of the sense of smell and taste, and swollen eyelids. The infection may also produce purulent greenish discharge due to bacterial infection. Fever and a high white blood cell count will follow. Other complaints include sore throat, headache, bad breath, nose bleeds, and general tiredness. The sinus infection can also spread to the lower air passage in the lung to cause chronic cough and bronchitis.

In clinical practice, chronic sinusitis is a common illness. The first line of treatment is medication. When purulent sinusitis occurs, there will be a stinking discharge. Acupuncture is a very dramatic remedy. With needling on the face, the discharge will drain from the nose; it will drain out completely in 12 hours. Such treatments are only effective in suppressing the symptoms. The disease will recur. If the patient has two attacks within a month, I would advise him or her to try Qigong exercise.

Case 1

I recall someone with a typical case of chronic sinusitis who came for Qigong in 1990. The lady had suffered from this disease for more than 35 years, starting when she was about 10. The sinusitis started with a lot of thin, nasal discharge and sneezing in the morning. She would have pain around the eyes coupled with a headache, which usually lasted until noon. Medication helped to control the symptoms and the drugs had to be taken regularly.

At times, mechanical irrigation and aspiration of the sinus had to be done weekly. This sinusitis eventually developed into persistent bronchitis that lasted for months. X-rays of the chest in 1985 showed a cyst in the middle right lobe of the lung. A benign cyst was removed surgically.

The operation did not ease the bronchitis, which later developed into bronchial asthma. Despite medication, this persisted for six months. In desperation, and with little confidence, she joined my class in 1990.

She was assigned a standard Kong Jing Qigong schedule (refer to section on CFS) with an additional 15 hours for the Horse Stance Posture, and an additional 25 hours for Arms Embracing Moon sequence (which mainly circulates the qi in the nose and lungs).

She continued the medication at the beginning of the Qigong treatment and gradually began to have no need of it. Her condition improved gradually in about six months. The asthma, nasal discharge, sneezing, headaches, and eye pain were completely eradicated. No medicine was required any longer. Her complexion improved and she appeared more energetic and cheerful.

The Horse Stance Posture is important in building up qi, which is led to the diaphragm after each exercise to be stored. When the qi becomes very strong, it is then returned to the nose and lungs through the palm (if the person practises the Arms Embracing Moon procedure).

The qi or energy helps to regulate the circulation in the nose and lungs, producing an anti-inflammatory and anti-allergic effect. It also acts on the bronchial tree of the lung to activate the cilia of the mucous lining of the bronchial tubes and sinuses. This in turn will sweep the secretion to the mouth from where it is coughed out of the respiratory system, relieving the cough due to bronchitis and sinusitis. The effect is immediate. As the lady was doing the exercise, the sputum was coughed out after 10 minutes.

Case 2

I had another case of chronic sinusitis four years after my first case. This was a professional who had had sinusitis for about two years. Eventually, fluid filled the left maxillary sinus. He was scheduled for an operation. Two weeks before, he learned that surgery might not cure the sickness and that the recurrence rate was very high. He came to me and began practising Qigong. After more than a month, the fluid drained itself out. He felt well and when he went for a follow-up visit to the ENT specialist, it was confirmed that surgery was not necessary.

Case 3

My third case of chronic sinusitis was a 15-year-old student who had had it for more than a year. In the few months prior to seeing me, his eyes became very tired around 10 a.m. to 11 a.m. and this was associated with headaches. His father had to fetch him home to rest. I saw him in my clinic for a few sessions and gave him the standard treatment and acupuncture as well. The therapeutic effect was temporary. Eventually, I advised him to join my class in August 1999. He practised the first two procedures of Kong Jing Qigong. By the third week, he no longer needed to go home in the morning to rest. The sinusitis cleared up in two months. He told me that he had gained an extra bonus from the exercise. His concentration power had improved and so had his memory.

C. Migraine

Migraine is defined as a familial disorder characterized by recurrent attacks of headache. The attacks are widely variable in intensity, frequency, and duration.

Migraine is much more prevalent than CFS. According to the *Journal of the American Medical Association* (1993), about 18 million Americans experienced severe migraine headaches and 4.5 million suffered more than one migraine attack each month. This disorder occurs more frequently in women. It varies with age, peaking in women between 35 and 40 years of age. About 75 percent of patients have a family history. If the first migraines occur after 40 years of age, it is essential to rule out any organic diseases by CT scan (computerized tomography scan, a diagnostic tool) and magnetic resonance image (MRI).

The cause of migraine is still unknown. But it is now recognized that it is due to a dysfunction of the brain involving neurological and biochemical changes.

The headaches are neither life-threatening nor a direct cause of death. But it is a painful, exhausting, and humiliating illness. There is no external sign to show how grave the situation is for a patient who has migraine. The patient is often unsympathetically stigmatized as having it "all in his head," implying that it is more of a psychological problem.

Migraine attacks may be moderate to incapacitating in intensity. The attacks may occur once a year or several times a week. But do note that it does not occur daily. An acute attack may last from four to 24 hours and most likely take place between 6 a.m. and 10 a.m. Many also occur at night.

A main sign of migraine is a pounding and throbbing pain which is usually unilateral at the onset. It may later radiate to the opposite side of the head. During the attack, the patient will appear pale and sick, is sweaty, with cold clammy hands, and have a feeling of tenderness in the scalp accompanied by pressing pain. The temporal artery on the side of the forehead may appear dilated and may pulsate. In fact, during the headache phase, all the body systems are directly affected. The patient may experience nausea and vomit, have diarrhea, and find food intolerable. Nasal congestion and a running nose occur often. Often, he will also be sensitive to light, noise, and odor. Thus he becomes more irritable and depressed, and has difficulty concentrating.

Before the onset of a headache, the patient may have a peculiar sensation called an aura, which lasts for 15 to 20 minutes. The most common symptoms are visual (e.g. seeing flashing lights, sparks, and blind spots). Other signs of aura include paresthesia (an unhealthy sensation over the body). Giddiness, faintness, and oversensitivity to smell will occur. These particular symptoms usually disappear before the headache phase.

Treatment

In modern medicine, there is no known cure for migraines. The object of treatment is to adjust the patient's lifestyle to minimize the frequency and severity of the attacks. Migraine patients are encouraged to form an association to help each other to cope with and better manage the illness.

The main treatment is to suppress or shorten each headache as it arises. Prophylactic measures to lessen future attacks have been a failure as the side effects of some of the drugs are very common; of these, the formation of fibrous tissue in the chest and abdomen is considered the worst. Operations may be needed to remove the fibrosis.

In my years of practice and study, I used medicine, acupuncture, and Qigong exercise to help my patients manage their migraines. After numerous trials, I am convinced that Qigong exercise is the treatment of choice. It may take weeks or months to get results, but it does offer a cure. I have treated a number of patients more than five years ago and no one has experienced a recurrence.

Case

A young, married woman working in the media industry had suffered from severe migraines for four to five years. At the peak, she experienced severe migraine attacks twice a week, each lasting about three hours. The attacks would usually occur at night.

Over the years, she realized that certain things would trigger a migraine within her. They were food and beverages like cheese, smoked fish, Ajinomoto, and coffee. Flickering lights, cigarette smoke, noise, and stress (a prime factor) also provoked a headache. There was no aura or visual disturbance but the mood change was apparent. During an attack, she would feel a chill and be more sensitive to noise. At times, she would feel giddy and nauseous, close to vomiting. To lessen the effects she anticipated, she would shut herself in a dark and quiet room.

After the attack, her skull would remain tender and this was accompanied by exhaustion and depression. She had to rest for another few hours because any physical exertion could cause a throbbing headache.

She had been taking medication without much improvement. In 1993, her migraines became very severe and frequent. She felt so sick and depressed that she had to apply for special unpaid sick leave to rest for a year. This in turn did not help much and she joined my class as a last resort. From what I could see, she looked really pale and tired and had cold hands.

I started her on the standard schedule of half an hour of exercise daily. Each procedure would last 15 hours. As she gradually improved, I added another 15 hours for the Horse Stance Posture, 5 hours for the Arms Embracing Moon exercise, and another 5 hours to regulate qi through the three entry points.

The Horse Stance Posture mainly serves to build up qi. It appears that the qi thus produced has a stabilizing and sedative effect on the brain. An independent scientific study shows that qi can produce an electrical wave very similar to that of sleeping humans. Sleep is essential for repairing tissues, which is effected by the production of growth hormones in the brain. Sleep also promotes the production of serotonin and endorphin, which are needed for the control of pain.

I had a patient with a case of mild migraine who practised the Horse Stance Posture alone for two months and was relieved of his headaches. When asked to continue the rest of the Qigong schedule, he declined. He claimed that getting rid of the headaches was enough for him. If the headaches returned he would just carry out the Horse Stance procedure.

Anyway, our lady practised the exercise conscientiously, as it was her last resort. In about two months, she was able to stop taking medicine and managed to have better sleep without any recurring headaches. However, about a month later, she had a headache, though it was not quite severe. I consider this a rebound phenomenon. It occurs in a number of patients with chronic diseases practising Qigong. I instructed her not to be bothered by this but to carry on with the exercise. In a few days, the pain disappeared without the use of medicine and has not returned since.

After about a year of practising Kong Jing Qigong, she stopped altogether, as she felt very healthy.

D. Ménière's Disease

This is the case of a middle-aged woman suffering from recurrent vertigo with pressure in the right ear, which always caused vomiting. She also had tinnitus (a ringing noise in the ear), which persisted with varying intensity. Hearing in that ear fluctuated.

She was admitted to the general hospital in Kuching on three occasions due to severe giddiness and vomiting. An ENT examination failed to reveal an abnormality, and a CT scan showed no lesion in the brain. She was diagnosed as having Ménière's Disease and was given various combinations of medicines, including Methycobal Vastarel, Stuperon, Diamox, Merislon, Tanakan, Mogadon, and Stemetil. The vertigo and vomiting persisted.

Her ENT surgeon in Sarawak referred her to an ENT surgeon in Singapore, who confirmed the diagnosis of Ménière's Disease. The medicines Merislon, Tanakan, and Stemetil were continued, and endolymphatic surgery was suggested if the condition did not improve. An endolymphatic sac operation was performed six months later after the vertigo, vomiting, and hearing loss became progressively worse. The sac was found to be dilated, with numerous blood vessels on the surface. After the operation, her hearing improved but she was still troubled by an unbearable floating sensation and balance problems, despite continued medication.

She came to me one month after the operation, looking pale, exhausted, and miserable. I started her with Kong Jing Qigong exercise. In her case, it was more important to reestablish the homeostasis of the body systems and to stabilise the internal environment of her body, especially the brain. I prescribed a Qigong schedule for the general building up of qi and regulation of the various organs through the jing luoh system. This was carried out daily for half an hour.

1. Horse Stance Posture	30 minutes daily, total:	15 hours
2. Arms Embracing the Moon		15 hours
3. Fostering the Primordial Qi		15 hours
4. Holding the Ball		15 hours
5. Rolling the Ball		15 hours
6. Regulating Qi Through Three Entry Points		15 hours

She experienced the rebound phenomenon (a reappearance of the symptoms) one month after beginning practice, and the symptoms lasted for 10 days. After that there was a gradual improvement of her condition. In five to six months she was feeling quite normal and gradually discontinued her medication over a further few months.

E. Sciatica, Prolapsed Disc

This case of low backache and sciatica pain in the right leg is very interesting. The patient, an elderly Chinese woman, very active and well preserved, complained of low backache radiating to the right leg, which made squatting and climbing stairs agonising. She went to China for treatment and was found to have possibly a sequestrum (a piece of dead disc) between the lumbar 5th and the sacral 1st vertebrae (L5/S1). The L5/S1 disc had protruded to the right and backward, compressing the dura, the connective tissue lining the spinal cord. An L5/S1 facet joint block was recommended, but the operation was not done.

She returned to Malaysia, consulted a specialist in Kuala Lumpur, and was advised to have an operation. In view of her age then (she was 65), she hesitated and sought the opinion of a specialist in London. The specialist, after studying records of the previous investigations, did not think an operation would do her any good. She resorted to pain relievers and hypotensive drugs. (She had had hypertension for many years.)

She was introduced to me two years later by another woman who had also suffered from sciatica but was cured after Qigong exercise. I prescribed a schedule of Kong Jing Qigong exercise emphasising Holding the Ball and Rolling the Ball.

1. Horse Stance Posture	30 minutes daily, total:	15 hours
2. Arms Embracing the Moon		15 hours
3. Fostering the Primordial Qi		15 hours
4. Holding the Ball		30 hours
5. Rolling the Ball		30 hours
6. Regulating Qi Through Three Entry Points		15 hours

The Holding the Ball exercise is mainly to move the positive and negative phases of qi into equilibrium. Rolling the Ball uses the palms to radiate external qi to the lumbar sacral region, down to the knees. Both procedures strengthen the qi in the paravertebral muscles and give strong and more balanced support to the spine.

She had a mild rebound phenomenon for three weeks after the fifth week of exercise. The condition then improved gradually. After seven months of practice, the sciatica and lower backache disappeared. She now has no trouble climbing stairs. What made her even happier is that her high blood pressure, which had been resistant to medication, was also reduced with the same medication.

F. Rheumatoid Arthritis

Rheumatoid arthritis occurs mostly in women of middle age, an age when, just as they are anticipating enjoyment of the fruits of their hard work, painful joints make them invalids. It usually starts with pain in one or two joints and then other joints are affected. This case study concerns a retired civil servant who had been suffering from joint pain for seven years. The pain recurred frequently until her finger joints, wrist joints, and knee joints were deformed, swollen, and locked. Medication relieved her pain moderately until about four months before she was referred to me, when medicine no longer seemed to work.

She walked into my clinic with a slow, painful, and limping gait, looking pale and exhausted. The left knee joint was swollen and could not extend fully. She could not stand up for more than five minutes, which prevented her from practising Kong Jing Qigong.

Six acupuncture sessions at three-day intervals alleviated her knee joint pain sufficiently to allow her to stand for 10 minutes. Then the Kong Jing Qigong exercise started. I prescribed a schedule quite similar to that for sciatica, emphasizing the Horse Stance Posture, Holding the Ball, and Rolling the Ball. I gave her more time to practise the Horse Stance Posture as her health was quite poor and she needed to build up her energy.

1. Horse Stance Posture	30–40 minutes daily, total: 40 hours
2. Arms Embracing the Moon	15 hours
3. Fostering the Primordial Qi	15 hours
4. Holding the Ball	30 hours
5. Rolling the Ball	30 hours
6. Regulating Qi Through Three Entry Points	15 hours

To be effective, Qigong exercise must be carried out every day, and each practice session must continue for 30 minutes at least. Long-term suffering had made this patient a very disciplined and determined person. She started with 10 minutes of exercise each time, as this was the limit of her tolerance, but practised three times a day to make up the 30 minutes daily requirement. In the first two months she found the results very good, which gave her more confidence to practise for a longer time. In the third month she was able to practise for 40 minutes each time. Her determination paid off. I saw her twice a week in my class, and each time she had something exciting to tell me. In the third month of practice, she could get up from her bed without help.

As I observed her progress, I was very excited to notice that her wrist joint swelling had subsided by more than 50 percent and her spindle-shaped finger joints had disappeared completely in four months. Her face became rosy. Her fingers could move smoothly and she could extend them fully. She was so happy that she made a pleasure trip to England.

The rebound phenomenon came a bit late in her case. She had swelling of the thumb and index fingers and pain in her left knee, although it was not as bad as before, and the wrist joint remained normal. This occurred seven months after she started Qigong exercise and lasted about two months. Then slowly the condition improved further.

Conclusion

As modern medical workers, we are at a great advantage in being able to apply our knowledge of medical science to this ancient art of healing. I have used this knowledge in attempting to find the channel system in the fascia and to explain qi in the form of electricity. Another example is the post-herpes pain. The points in the Chinese text are not very helpful. But with the knowledge of the virus locating at the ganglion of the spinal nerve, I was able to "needle" the skin over the site of the affected nerve to relieve the pain almost completely.

Acupuncture and Qigong are still a mystery in the scientific world. It is only in the past few decades that interest in this ancient art of healing has been rekindled. Modern scientific studies have been carried out to enhance our understanding of qi and the channel system. It is an adventure that deserves our attention as it will reveal yet another system in our body which is beyond the reach of modern medicine. Greater knowledge of this system may further our understanding of our own body and help us to combat diseases with a better weapon in future.

Glossary

A

arrhythmia Deviation from the normal heart rhythm.

ascites Accumulation of fluid in peritoneal cavity.

ATP Adenosine triphosphate, a molecule in body cells that provides energy.

B

biofeedback The giving of immediate information to a subject about bodily processes that are usually unconscious, e.g. heart rate.

C

Chronic Fatigue Syndrome (CFS) A condition characterized by sleep disorders and disruption of the immune system.

conjunctivitis Inflammation of conjunctiva, the membrane covering the eye and lining the inside of eyelids.

cortisone Naturally occurring steroid hormone synthesized by the adrenal cortex. It functions primarily in carbohydrate metabolism and is used in the treatment of rheumatoid arthritis, adrenal insufficiency, certain allergies, and gout.

cosmic radiation A few thousand years ago, Chinese physicians postulated that the universe is filled with cosmic energy that carried a positive charge and the earth's magnetic field carried a negative charge; these two energies combine to create weather, seasons, day and night, and the five elements of metal, water, wood, fire, and earth to propagate plants and animals. In recent years, space satellites discovered that the earth is surrounded by a large swarm of highly charged atomic particles extending 50,000 miles out into space. A large number of these come from the sun and they are trapped by the earth's magnetic field, forming the "magnetosphere".

CT Computerised tomography, a method of diagnosis based on radiology combined with computer technology to give a cross-sectional image of soft body tissue.

D

dopamine Body chemical controlling the transmission of nerve impulses.

dorsum The back, upper, or posterior surface.

Down's syndrome A condition associated with a chromosomal abnormality and characterized by a small and flattened skull, short and flat-bridged nose, epicanthal fold, short phalanges, and widened space between the first and second digits of hand and foot, with moderate to severe mental retardation.

E

Electroencephalogram (EEG) A graphic record of brain waves.

endocrine Secreting internally, most commonly into the systemic circulation.

endorphin Chemical compound with pain-relieving properties.

ENT Commonly used abbreviation for Eye, Nose, and Throat.

erythema multiforme A disease caused by blood toxins manifested as lesions that look like rashes to appear suddenly on the face, neck, forearms, and legs.

external qi Qi in the body after strengthening by Qigong exercise and storage in the internal elixir of the abdomen. The qi is later sent out of the body by mind control to effect its therapeutic function in treating another person's sickness through the practitioner's channel.

F

fascia Connective tissue surrounding organs of the body. Superficial fascia is the tissue just beneath the skin.

G

ganglion A group of nerve cells forming a nerve centre, especially one located outside the brain or spinal cord.

gangrene Death of tissue usually in considerable mass and generally associated with loss of vascular supply and followed by bacterial invasion and putrefaction.

H

hemiplegia Paralysis of one side of the body.

herpes zoster (shingles) Viral attack causing pain in the affected nerve and sometimes an eruption of blisters on the skin.

histology Science of the minute structure of tissues and organs in relation to their function.

homeostasis A state in which all internal body systems are maintained at equilibrium regardless of changes in external conditions.

humerus Long bone of the arm or forelimb extending from the shoulder to the elbow.

hypertrophic Enlarged (organ or tissue) due to increase in size rather than the number of constituent cells.

hypothalamus The region of the forebrain linked with the thalamus above and the pituitary gland below.

I

iliacus Muscle in the groin.

interferon Substance produced by cells infected with a virus; it has the ability to inhibit viral growth.

ischaemia Insufficient flow of blood to a part of the body.

J

jing luoh Network of energy channels located in connective tissue called fascia, through which qi flows.

L

leukaemia Malignant disease of the blood-forming organs in which abnormal white cells are produced and normal blood cell production is suppressed, leading to anaemia, bleeding, and susceptibility to infections.

lumbar vertebrae Five bones in the lower part of the backbone.

M

Ménière's Disease Disease affecting inner ear causing deafness and vertigo.

menorrhagia Heavy menstrual bleeding.

mesentery Membrane containing blood, nerves, and lymph vessels that attaches abdominal organs (including the stomach, small intestine, pancreas, and spleen) to the back wall of the abdomen.

mitochondria Small spherical to rod-shaped components found in the cytoplasm of cells, enclosed in a double membrane, the inner one having infoldings called cristae. They are the principal sites of the generation of energy, in the form of ion gradients and adenosine triphosphate (ATP) synthesis, resulting from oxidation of foodstuffs.

moxibustion Treatment in which a herb is placed on skin at acupuncture points and ignited. For the same effect, moxa sticks are commonly used, with the burning end held close to the skin.

N

necrosis Death of body tissue.

neurones Nerve cells that transmit impulses, which is how information is conveyed through the nervous system.

O

occiput Back of the head.

oedema Accumulation of fluid in body tissue.

P

parasympathetic Relating to or affecting the autonomic nervous system originating in the brain stem and the lower part of the spinal cord.

pericardium Membranous covering of heart.

perineum The area between the anus and the genital organs.

peristalsis Wave-like movement of tubes such as the intestines that cause their contents to be pushed forward.

peritoneum Serous membrane of the abdominal cavity.

pleural cavity Space between the visceral pleura covering lungs and the parietal pleura covering the inner surface of the chest wall.

porolactic Pertaining to the pituitary hormone that stimulates and maintains the secretion of milk.

Ω

qi Energy or life force responsible for health and growth.

R

recticulum A fine network formed by cells, certain structures within cells, or connective tissue fibres between cells.

rhinitis Inflammation of the mucous membrane of the nose.

S

sacrum Five fused bones forming a triangular shape in the backbone. The sacrum lies below the lumbar bones and above the coccyx, which is the tail end of the backbone.

somatic muscle There are three structurally different types of muscle tissue: skeletal, cardiac, and visceral. Skeletal muscle is attached to various bones of the skeleton and is known also as somatic muscle. *Soma* means body, and somatic muscle involves all the muscles in the body wall.

Stephen-Johnson syndrome A severe form of erythema multiforme with lesions in the oral and anogenital mucous membranes, accompanied by malaise, prostration, headache, fever, joint pain, and conjunctivitis.

T

transmutation The changing of an atomic nucleus to one of a different number, causing a rearrangement of protons and neutrons.

triple warmer A term used mostly by Taiwanese writers, Sanjiao in Chinese. It concerns the lining of internal body cavities: the pleural cavity enclosing the lungs and heart; and the peritoneal cavity enclosing all the organs of the abdomen. The Triple Warmer is divided into three sections: the upper section is the pleural cavity; the middle section is the upper abdominal cavity containing the spleen and stomach; and the lower section is the lower abdominal cavity containing the liver, kidneys, urinary bladder, and large and small intestines.

V

viscera The soft internal organs of the body, especially those contained within the abdominal and thoracic cavities.

Y

yin and yang Two complementary poles of energy. In Chinese philosophy, yin is negative, dark, and feminine while yang is positive, bright, and masculine.

Index